Fifty Shades of Pink

a parody

Faythe America

Published in the United States
Copyright © 2012 Faythe America
All rights reserved.

America, Faythe
    Fifty Shades of Pink: A Parody/Faythe America. —1st ed.
    Summary: Maggie is a klutz. Mr. Pink is an ass. When she falls into his office, it's love. Well, sort of. Unfortunately, this enigmatic billionaire has a dark, dangerous, unspeakable secret. What will innocent Maggie do when she discovers the man who has stolen her heart is hiding something...pink?
    ISBN-13: 978-1478212270
    ISBN-10: 1478212276
    [1. E. L. James. 2. Fifty Shades of Gray—Parodies, imitations, etc. 3. Humor—Erotica.] I. Title

What people are saying about
Fifty Shades of Pink

"Drunk Faythe America is *not* drunk Hemingway!" —*old white man's corpse that washed up from the sea*

"I'll never be able to look at a snuggly the same way again!" —*Irreparably scarred individual*

"This book should be taught in teen abstinence programs." —*Someone who will probably never have sex again*

"WTF was the author on?" —*Someone who REALLY wants to know*

"I'm glad to know I wasn't the only person traumatized by your sex scenes, Faythe." —*Faythe's best friend after reading one of her many 1-star reviews.*

"I'm so proud of you for writing a book! Now, whatever you do, don't tell your father." —*Faythe's Mom*

Read if you dare...

PROLOGUE

PINK. IT'S THE COLOR OF innocence, or at least that's what you're supposed to believe. Little girls wear pink dresses with pink frills, play with pink dolls, and eat cupcakes adorned with pink frosting and sparkles. I know because I was once one of those little girls. I thought that pink is the color of fairy tales and saccharine dreams.

I was wrong.

Pink is really the color of salvation and sin. Of pain and ecstasy.

It's the name of the man who would introduce me to a world I'd never dreamed possible.

A world you can never leave once you've tasted its forbidden pleasures.

Even if staying destroys you.

1

M R. PINK'S TOWER STOOD erect in the center of the city, as pink as his namesake. According to the rumors, it was so freaking huge that you could see it from space. A year ago, some upstart named *Monsieur Gris* had tried to build a bigger skyscraper. Mr. Pink did not let that challenge stand...unchallenged. Immediately, he organized his cabal of underpaid Mexican immigrants to make his skyscraper bigger. Better. Meatier.

Well, *Monsieur Gris'* puny tower took one look at Mr. Pink's epic size and crumbled to the ground. All that was left of the conquered man's valiant efforts was the skeleton of a building, a sea of noxious ash, and one man's broken dream. Yeah, that's right; Mr. Pink *ate shit* like that *for breakfast*. He then bought the pile of rubble and left it in its pathetic state to warn any who might dare to try to cockblock him again.

A shiver shot through me. Damn, the man was ruthless! But you couldn't fault his business acumen, or his charitable nature. He let poor kids play at the building site. Well, after they'd received tetanus shots, of course, and signed a waiver stating that Mr. Pink was not liable for any damage their little bodies might sustain while monkey-baring up 300 feet of rusty metal that could collapse at any moment.

Fuck! Shit fuck! Collapse like me! Lordy, I'd been stuck in his teak and gold elevator for like fifteen minutes or something. I rolled my shoulders. Ugh! Charlie Horse! Even my ankles were cramping from standing so long. I mean, it took forever to get to the top, because again, *you could see this shit from space.* But the fact that he was willing to inconvenience everyone who wanted to talk to him, and himself every day when he went to work, was just proof of how this guy was *the shit.*

The elevator dinged and the doors slid open.

I screamed.

Sitting in front of me, at the pink desk in front of a lush, pink carpet, dressed in a revealing pink business suit, was some chick with the most glorious tits I'd ever seen. A little light pink lace peeked out around her cleavage. It made her look almost innocent, although this woman couldn't possibly be innocent. *Because she wore a unicorn mask over her head.*

The white horse mask stretched all the way down to her neck. Varying shades of pink hair sprouted from the mane. The horn was gold and...*Fuck!* I thought as I took a closer look. It had a freaking 14 karat stamp on it! That was a real gold horn!

Holy Macaroni!

"You must be Mr. Pink's two o'clock."

"Um, what?"

Unicorn Secretary groaned as she handed me a pink form. At the bottom of the form was a black rose.

Black rose? My heart skipped a beat. Who would have thought Mr. Pink was so deep? I mean, it was a flower, but it was black. Flowers weren't black. They were pretty colors. And his name was pink. Why was the rose the single black thing? *What did it mean????*

But before I could ponder this longer, Unicorn Secretary interrupted my thoughts. "Fill this out. He'll see you in a few minutes."

I leaned over and accepted the pen she handed me. It was carpeted in pink feathers, and had pink, feathery sparkles sprouting from the top. Damn, Mr. Pink was classy.

I looked down at the form.

"Oh, and make sure to sign here." Unicorn Secretary nodded her head, slapping the bottom part of the form with her horn.

I frowned. What was my favorite food? What was my favorite color? Did I like hot dogs? What was up with these questions? "Well, I will sign when I get to that part—"

"No! Now!" Unicorn Secretary neighed.

"Lady, look—"

Her chair clattered to the floor as she reared. She whinnied and slapped her horn down on the page again.

Wowsers!

"Okay, okay," I yelled, signing my name. My hand shook because her freaking horn was out of control, and it kept bonking my hand as she chanted: *sign! sign! sign!* Holy mother of shit-faced Christ, this bitch was crazy! "There!" I yelled! "I did what you asked! Are you happy!?"

She sat down, shook her head once, and folded her hands on the top of the desk. "Alright, Mr. Pink will see you now."

A shiver shot through my entire body.

The pink feathers on the pink quill seemed to quiver from the breeze—i.e. the air conditioner blasting fucking freezing air from the corner.

Fuck! I mean, super fuck! Why did I feel like I'd just signed away my fate?

"Through those doors," Unicorn Secretary said.

I nodded and opened them, but nothing in my 21 years on this planet could prepare me for what I discovered inside.

2

I RAN MY HANDS OVER my arms as I stepped into the room. It was cold. Ruthlessly, passionately cold. But not as ruthless, or passionate, or cold as the man seated before me in the pink leather chair.

It was said that the hearts of most women stopped for a second when they first laid eyes on Mr. Pink. Some women's hearts even stopped completely. He had a face that could kill. A face a woman would die for.

My left arm went numb. A searing pain shot through my chest as if I'd been stabbed. This dude gave heart breaker a whole new meaning!

He was ruggedly handsome, yet as lithe and graceful as David. The devastatingly sharp angles of his face were softened by his quirky, upturned lips. And those eyes...*hot diggity damn!* His eyes bore into me, as if he could see the deepest, darkest secrets of my soul.

Ha! Too bad I don't have any deep, dark secrets, dude! There's nothing going on upstairs at all!

"Miss America?"

Double fuck! His voice was so hot! Like a roid raging *The Bat-Man*. I began to claw at my chest, and buttons popped off like a machine gun fire.

"Miss America?" He repeated.

"Ughhhh!" I moaned, shutting my eyes. Good thing I'd come prepared by wearing three shirts! *Ha again!* So many girls started stripping once they saw Mr. Pink that I'd decided to come prepared! I ripped off my top shirt and gave it a few victory waves around my head before tossing it off to the side.

It was also said that most girls fainted when they saw Mr. Pink.

Well, I wasn't like most girls. *I* didn't faint.

Instead, I belly flopped onto the floor.

The pink rug was cushy, but my head still pounded as my chin slammed into the ground. *Triple whammy fuck!* The papers containing my interview questions floated around me. *Quadruple whammy fuck fest!*

"Miss America, are you alright?" He sounded bored. I guess he was used to women hemorrhaging in front of him.

My arms kept giving out each time I tried to sit up, as if I were a car whose battery had died, and my brain kept stabbing the key into the ignition, swearing and screaming and hoping to God someone with car jacks would stop and get her running again.

Did Mr. Pink have car jacks?

No wait! I couldn't ask him! Then he'd know what affect he had on me!

I leaped up, put my hand on my hip, smiled, and said: "Nice rug you got there," like I'd planned the whole thing.

He frowned.

Ha! Totally fooled him! Good one! Then I snickered, because nothing is more awesome than laughing at your own jokes.

"Are you alright, Miss America?"

"Oh yeah, dude…" I trailed off. Something was wrong. But what is it?

"Would you like a seat, Miss America?"

A little light bulb turned on inside my head. *Literally.* Because that's totally anatomically possible. *Oh, the irony.* Wait, why did that light bulb turn on again? Oh yeah! I just remembered! "Hey, I am *not* Miss America!"

"Oh?" He raised his brow. "And who might you be, then?"

"I might be Maggie. I mean, not might be. That's my name and stuff."

"Maggie," he repeated, with a quirk of his lips.

"Yeah. Maggie Sterling. As in *silver.*" I cocked out my hip to show my attitude, then leaned over shuffled the papers but did not pick them up. "Faythe is sick. She was totally gross and crusty this morning. Puked everywhere like it was Niagara Falls."

Mr. Pink's face turned green. "Excuse me?"

"Anyways, she gave me the questions. I'm just gonna rattle them off and tape them for her, is that alright?"

"That's fine," he said. "You know, I don't usually allow these sorts of things to be taped."

"Oh? Well, thanks, I guess."

"I'm making an exception for you," he said after a dramatic pause.

"Cool-e-o." I decided that I'd shuffled the papers enough so I fumbled them for a few moments. Then, after I'd given myself my tenth paper cut, I decided to pick them up. They were all out of order, but what did I care?

I stood, and then grimaced. *Fuckery!* What was wrong with me today? Immediately, I looked at the mirror hanging conveniently on his wall, because I realized I hadn't described my physical appearance yet.

Ugh! I almost cried out when I saw my face!

My lips were too pouty. My eyes too large and far apart. Also, way too blue, like a perfect, cloudless summer day. My skin too porcelain. My head too heart-shaped. And that nose! Ugh! Cute as a *freaking button*!

I looked away in disgust, shaking my wavy, brown hair that refused to be tamed. Silky, sexy tendrils flopped over my face and breasts. *Burning shit on the sidewalk!* Why were my breasts so damn perky? What did they have to be so happy about? It wasn't their fucking birthday. And why did they have to bounce around when I walked and stuff?

I glanced over at Mr. Pink.

Now that I no longer suffered from heart palpations, I could take in my surroundings. Everything in the room was the palest shade of pink, save for him. *He* was dressed in vibrant, mesmerizing pink. And yeah, he totally rocked the salmon shirt. *Hot diggity dog*, he was the hottest thing I'd ever seen.

"Are you ready, Miss Sterling?"

Light streamed through the double windows, casting his body in black. He looked like the devil incarnate himself. As if on cue, two doves flew from the window behind him. Then two crows, cawing. Then, a bald eagle soared past.

Wowsers! Mr. Pink was nothing if not an American. *And* he knew how to rock a salmon shirt!

But seriously, I couldn't let his patriotism or his sexiness distract me. Black rose! Doves! Crows! It was like the universe was trying to tell me something through clichéd biblical imagery! But what did it mean? And why was none of it pink?

"Miss Sterling, you have done nothing but stare at me for the past three minutes."

Oh fuck! "Oh, uh…"

He lowered his voice. "Do you have things on your mind *other* than our interview?"

"No, of course not. I'm super dependable, and a real-time thinker." Yeah! I remembered to use a big word! And even added something else that sounded super good. I cleared my throat and read off the first question on the page. "Have you ever been with a man?"

"What?"

My eyes went wide. Was that really the question? *Oh my! Dearest me!* "I mean, have you ever done a business deal with a man before. You know, not sexual stuff but like, business stuff…" I babbled.

He frowned. "Yes. I've done business deals with men before."

I swallowed. "Oh really? Wow. How did they go?"

"Depends on the deal and who I was working with."

"Oh, that's nice," I whispered. Time for a new question. I wet my lips as I started the next. "Have you ever checked out a guy's ass?"

"I beg your pardon?"

I looked down at the paper. Was that really what was written? "I mean…" I fumbled. The papers fell to the floor. *Again.* Oh God, what if he read what was on them? There was only one thing I could do!

I jumped up on my chair.

Mr. Pink's eyes bugged out of his head. "Miss Sterling!"

Paying him no heed, I swan dove over the papers. Once I hit, I started doing the butterfly, because even though it's not the most graceful swim stroke, it sure sounds pretty.

"Miss Sterling?" He asked, obviously worried he'd allowed a crazy woman into his office.

I had to think of something fast! "That's not what I mean. I mean. That's not it. I mean,"

"Yes?"

"I mean, you have a nice ass," I said.

Worst. Cover. Up. Ever.

"You think I have a nice ass?" He repeated slowly.

"Uh, yeah." I whispered to the carpet.

"I'm surprised, Miss Sterling."

Oh, the fact that he was surprised totally didn't surprise me.

"Look, I'm not normally like this," I said, shooting up. I grabbed the questions in a wad and stuffed them behind my back.

He touched his lips. "Oh? That's a bit disappointing." Before I could make sense of that, he continued. "That's not what I was surprised by, though, Miss Sterling."

"Oh, then what was it?"

"It was that you haven't seen my ass yet."

I felt all the blood drain out of my face. "What?"

"I mean, you haven't seen my ass yet. I've been sitting down this entire time." He tilted his head to the side. "Unless, of course, you've seen it before at some point."

"No, I've never seen anyone like you. I'd remember if I did."

"Of course you would." He smiled, as if he was sharing a secret with me. "So, is that why you were on the floor?"

"Is what why?"

"So you could get a better look."

I had a sinking feeling I didn't like where this was going. "A better look?" I choked.

"Yes. A better look at my ass."

At that moment, I died a little. And not the kind of "little death" that the French talk about in their orgasms. I mean fifty tons of steel dropped on my head. Fifty tigers ripped my body to shreds. Fifty feathers tickled my remains, giving me, in my last moments, fifty kinds of agony.

And I think, right at that second, that my cheeks turned fifty shades of pink.

Goodness gracious! I had to stop this! But I couldn't think of how to reverse the situation with my mind powers. So I reached for a paper and read the first question I saw. "Have you ever been gagged?"

I should really know better than to keep reading stuff off this list of questions. Stupid, stupid! But I didn't know what to say!

He leans back, expression thoughtful. "Why? Do you want to gag me, Maggie?"

"No," I squeaked.

"These are oddly specific questions."

"Well, you know Faythe," I said, then realized he actually didn't know Faythe. "Well," I began again, "she has specific interests."

"I'd feel more comfortable answering these questions if I knew they wouldn't be appearing in your friend's thesis paper." He leaned forward, eyes locking on mine in challenge. "In fact, I think it's a little odd that a her thesis would require me to comment on my own ass."

"Oh," I murmured. That was kind of weird.

Still…it's probably a nice ass…

"If you want, we could go someplace private and discuss a few things…off the record."

"That isn't necessary!" I blurted out, suddenly hot. Hell, who was I kidding? I'd been hot since this interview started. "I mean, I'm sure she meant had you ever been gagged on something like a legal document."

"No one has ever thrust legal documents down my throat before."

"Metaphorical legal document!" I said. "No, wait, metaphorical gagging. Like, you know. A simile or some shit. Like, your eagerness to write up this legal document was like a dog gagging on his treats."

"I have to admit I'm extremely confused, Maggie."

"So am I! And I'm the one who has to live inside this brain!"

He raised a brow. "Touché."

I blew air out my mouth. "Indeed." Alright. Time to get sophisticated. Otherwise he'd think I was a freak! Aha! There was one that sounded pretty damn smarto. "Have you ever teabagged someone?"

He blanched.

I looked at the teapot in between us. "I guess I can put that down as a yes. I really like tea too, you know, and sometimes you do have to dip the bag up and down in the pot to get all the flavor out…"

"No, wait Miss—"

"It's alright. I like tea more than coffee too." I winked. "I'll never tell."

"That isn't what I was getting at—"

"Have you ever given someone a rim job?"

He started choking.

I tapped my pencil on the side of the paper. "You know, I'm a car mechanic. Actually, how could you know that? Ha ha ha…anyways, I think Faythe meant something else, but what could it be? I know," I grinned, leaning forward. "Have you ever given your car a lube job? No wait, have you ever cleaned its pipes? Have you ever...I can't figure out if she was talking about the gas tank or the engine."

"Miss Sterling..."

"Wait a minute," I said, frowning. Something wasn't adding up. "All these questions are kinda, well...what I'd really want to know is about how you're such a fucking stud in the boardroom. So, tell me about your business plan."

"Business plan?" He laughed. "I don't need a business plan, sweetheart."

"Wow! Really?"

"Yes. I just walk into each transaction believing that the other party will bend to my will, and they always do."

"Hot diggity dog!"

"There are many reasons why my opponents call me...*ballsy*... Miss Sterling."

"Wowsers! You must have freaking eight pound bowling balls!"

He grinned. "They're pretty fucking epic. Whenever I close a deal, I just slap my junk down on the table and stare down everyone with the alpha glare."

Oh geese! I mean, oh gees! We aren't migrating for the winter any time soon! "Wow. Your junk?"

"Sometimes the Pink Hammer is mightier than the pen *and* the sword." He smirked.

Pink Hammer! I wonder what he whacked with it! "Damn! Remind me to never play whack-a-mole with you!"

His smirk deepened. "You're a smart girl, Miss Sterling. But if I should ever get a chance to play a game of whack-a-mole for certain stakes—say, strip whack-a-mole—then no, I shan't remind you if you decide to enter into the devil's dance with me."

Devil's Dance? *Oh gosh.* He couldn't possibly mean…

Some part, deep inside me, began to loosen. As if a freaking happy face flower inside me was blooming, coaxed by the subtle passion laced in his tone…

I couldn't move for a second. What had he just said? Dude, what the fuck? Was he…was he….Oh damn, the way he looked at me was so freaking HOT! And, what was I doing? Why couldn't I think?

Mr. Pink's lips curled into a Cheshire smile. "Do you want to dance with me, Miss Sterling, like silver?"

Shiver me timbers! What the fucking damn? *I mean…oh my goodness!*

"Miss Sterling…" he leaned forward, offering me a hand. "You look a little pink."

That snapped me out of his siren's spell. *God! Me so stupid!* How could I fall for a man with such a devastating smile, such devastating eyes, such devastating…?

Alright, I had a reason, but what the fuck? I jumped up, my lips moving up and down in flustered motions because, *hot damn!* I was flustered! "Mr. Pink…I…I…I…FUCK!" I turned and ran. Really, what else could I do? I mean, it wasn't like he was ever going to think about me again. I'd totally gone freaky wow on his ass!

But Mr. Pink wasn't done with me.

He wasn't even close.

3

I LIVE IN THE DORMS WITH my bff-forever (yes, that's best-friends-forever-forever), Faythe. She's a total slut, but that's okay because she pays two-thirds of the rent. "So, how did the interview go?" Faythe asked as she swirled a tub of ruby lipstick over the crack on her face.

I groaned and fell face first on my bed. Then I fisted my face. I mean, I rubbed my face with my hands. Hey! People totally do that! Don't look at me that way!

Anyways, back to the present—or should I say, the present in past tense. I glanced over at Faythe and said: "Horrible."

"Horrible?" Faythe asked. "How could it go bad?"

"What was up with those questions?"

"Oh, those." She paused. "They were real good, weren't they?"

"They were god awful!" I shrieked. "What the hell was up with all those questions about his ass?"

She grinned. Her voice dropped. "Was it hot?"

"Yes it was—wait, that isn't the point!"

She laughed. "You did good, Maggie. Let me see what you got."

I handed over the tape. She popped her ear buds in her ears, clicked the start button with her index finger, and put her head on her pillow. Wait, that didn't sound right. She put her pillow on her head? *Fuck! Mindfuck!* Anyways, she propped her feet up on the side of the bed. Then, she looked at me with her eyes. "This is really going to make things good."

"Wait," I murmured before handing her my written notes, "you don't seem sick."

"Oh, it wasn't anything big."

"Wasn't anything big? Then why did I just travel all that way to humiliate myself to interview him?"

"Don't get mad at me, Maggie."

"Oh my God. What did you do?"

"Nothing big," she evaded.

"Tell me, or I'm taking back this tape!" I dove for it.

She squealed and stood on the bed, and then started jumping up and down. She held the tape above her head, and kicked her feet at me, as if I'd tackle her.

"What did you do?" I demanded.

"Alright," she said, a bit breathless from all the jumping. "I wasn't sick."

"Oh really? Then why the hell did I go?"

"I didn't think I could ask him such personal questions."

"Uh huh."

"So I sent you because…well…when you are in front of someone you don't know you get really flustered, and I knew you'd just read whatever was on those sheets."

"I hate you."

"It's alright to hate me," she said as she stopped jumping. "But I am so thankful for this. I really needed it for my thesis."

I sighed. "Really? How are those questions going to help you with your final project?"

"Because I'm writing a yaoi fanfic."

"You're writing a yaoi fanfic for your final project in college? What the hell are you thinking! You can't turn in a fanfic!"

"Why not?"

"Because it's not something you did!"

"But I did do it," she said. Something dinged in the corner of our dorm. "Oh, pop tarts are ready! Do you want one?"

I watched the smoke rise from the toaster. Sparks flew. "Not really, because that toast has been in there for, like, fifteen minutes at least."

"What can I say? I like it well toasted."

Charcoal flakes burst out of her mouth as she gobbled it down. "You really need to get out more, Maggie."

"You need to look at yourself in the mirror," I grumbled back.

I grabbed my bag and stuck my foot in my flip-flops. I was about to make my grand exit, and yes, it would have been grand. Faythe's hoodie was hanging on the door. I could have let it fall when I opened it, and then stepped on it, and then kicked it, and as I kicked it I could have accidentally kicked one of my flip-flops off as well, and I could storm off with only one flip-flop all pissed, and then have to come back for the other because *Damn!* It's hard to walk around with only one shoe on, ya know? Especially when that shoe is a lonely flip-flop that has no other friend in the world except the other flip-flop, which I so heartlessly kicked away. Wow, what a fucking tragedy, but life is like that sometimes.

Anyways.

None of that happened. This is what we like to call a meaningless segue in a novel. (By the way, it took me 21 years to learn how to spell segue. I still actually don't know if that's right.)

Anyways. Again.

That's when the phone rang.

BRING! BRING! BRING! DING-A-LING-A-LING! Then, the "thong song" ring tone started blasting and Faythe swayed her hips and hee-yawed until she reached the phone.

But she was too late.

She missed the phone.

Our message started playing.

Faythe Answering Machine: Hello? What's up?

"Hello. Is Miss Sterling available?"

Faythe Answering Machine: "Who did you say this was again?"

"I didn't. This is Mr. P—"

Faythe Answering Machine: "Hello? Hello?"

"Hello? Oh, it looks like the connection—d"

Faythe Answering Machine: "HELLO?"

"One second, I'll call back."

Faythe Answering Machine: "Hahahahahaha! This was just the answering machine! Leave a message after tha beep, SUCKER!"

Mr. Pink sighed. "Really, that is so bloody juvenile."

I fumed. Did she think she was freaking *British* now? That *two timing slut!* Oh wait, that was Mr. Pink who said that. Not Faythe.

Well damn. I should learn to read better.

Anyways, the message beep—you know, *that beep*—beeped.

Mr. Pink sighed again. "Hello Miss America," he boomed, irritation in his voice evident. "I turned down your offer for a photo shoot when you first asked for an interview."

Faythe went still.

"However, I am willing to reconsider your proposal, if little Miss Sterling is part of the show."

4

ALL OF JONAS' FAMILY ARE lumberjacks. He usually spends about 90% of his time with his shirt off, *"because his shirt just can't handle how sexy his abs are."* Well, it's kind of true. Everyone knows lumbermen cut down trees bareback, because there's nothing like the feeling of wood chips slicing your perfectly defined muscles to remind you that you're alive.

Anyways, Jonas and I have been friends for a very long time. I mean, we haven't known each other long enough to be childhood friends exactly, since we met in High School, but we are super close. Jonas is always there for me, regardless of whether I want to talk about my favorite new pair of shoes at 2am, or to drive me to my new boyfriend's house—though he can be a pain to drive with sometimes because he keeps sniffling and saying silly things like: *"that guy isn't nearly good enough for you, Maggie!"* But I know he just says things like that because we are really great friends! He's looking out for me!

Awwwww! Cutie boy! I flicked one of Jonas' nipples. *Right back at ya, dynamite!* "Thanks for doing this," I say as I bite my lower lip.

Jonas' eyes softened. "Well, someone had to."

"Yeah, but you're the only one I asked," I whispered.

"Only because you knew I'd never turn you down." He stepped forward, grabbing my hands. "Never."

Before I could answer, the door opened.

I spun around, forgetting Jonas the second I see Mr. Pink.

That fucking stud dropped his coat on the floor. "Miss Sterling," he purred as his assistant picked up his coat and placed it on a hanger. "So good to see you."

"Um, uh, hi."

"Is this the guy I'm supposed to pose with?" Jonas said, stepping forward.

Mr. Pink raised his brows. "Do I sense a challenge?"

Jonas grabbed the elastic band on his shorts and snapped it. "You're on, boy."

Whoa! "What's going on, you two?" I put my hands on my hips and tilted my head to the side.

Jonas immediately blushed. "Sorry Maggie."

Mr. Pink snorted. "You allow buffoons like this to be on a first-name basis with you, Miss Sterling?"

Jonas scowled. "I didn't ask, asshole. Normal people use people's names, dude."

Mr. Pink's lips began to twitch. "Normal people," he repeated, voice as dark as a million black suns as he turned to face me. "Well, now I can see why you're silver instead of gold!"

What? I wasn't gonna take that! Even if I was silver instead of Gold!

So I slapped him. *Jesus being nailed to the fucking cross double crap!* The sound was so loud that it was like I had a freaking fish attached to my hand! *Can I get a what-what!*

Wait! Supernova no-no bro! I'd just slapped the most important man in the entire city! A freaking billionaire! And I'd done it in front of some guy with his shirt off!

"Oh no you didn't!" Jonas squealed. "Dude, he's gonna go ape-shit on you! Duck and roll!"

Mr. Pink glared at Jonas. "No, I'm not that kind of man." He pressed his hand to where I'd struck him and shut his eyes. Slowly, his tongue peeked out from between his lips, a sliver of pink against his creamy skin. It moved from side to side as his eyes opened.

His pupils were dilated, as if drugged. His lips parted a little further. They seemed to hold some promise he wouldn't dare speak. But his eyes communicated it—the darkness in them, the passion, as if it were about to consume me entirely until I was nothing but molten gold in his hands.

"You're very forward, Miss Sterling," he said, voice husky.

Well pardon me good sir. My girly parts jingled like holiday bells on the door of the mall the day after Christmas.

Just then, Faythe coughed. She had her arms crossed over her chest. I gave her the super mad glare, and the corner of her mouth quirked up. "So glad you could make it, Mr. Pink."

"I always keep my engagements," was Mr. Pink's smooth answer. Then, he glanced at me.

Holy hog dogs! No, wait. That look was so padded it could have been a corn dog!

Faythe nodded to a woman to her right. I'm not gonna describe her because...she basically has no part in this story. I mean, I really want to have to avoid describing women other than totally-relatable-me and my slutty-best-friend who's supposed to make me look better by comparison.

"This insignificant secondary character shall do your make up, good sir." Faythe said, fluttering her eyelashes.

"Dude! What the fuck!" Jonas yelled, throwing up his hands.

"What a simpleton," Mr. Pink cooed, "who doesn't understand class." He kissed Faythe's hand, and then glanced up at me with a smile.

Crapola! It was like fifty Tasmanian devils had just been awakened in my stomach by necromancy and were exacting their revenge on little old me for my race's role in their extinction! *What the fuck was going on?*

Jonas stormed off.

"Good riddance, I say," Mr. Pink said.

"Well, it's a good thing you *don't* say," Faythe fired back. "This is a two-person photo-shoot, and he's you partner."

"YOU'RE SO GONNA THANK ME for this," Faythe muttered.

I shut my eyes and tried, for the fiftieth time that hour, to disappear. I mean, *freaking peeping-tom!* Shit was *going down* in the other room. Something about Mr. Pink refusing to put on a thermal band...

Faythe wiggled her eyebrows. "Don't play dumb. You know what I mean."

"I was not told this would be this kind of shoot," came Mr. Pink's voice. "It isn't usually until the first date that I let a girl get my clothes off."

There were giggles.

I felt my blood pressure spike. "Tell me again, Faythe. Why am I supposed to thank you?"

Before she could answer, the door swung open.

I blinked, almost blinded. *Holy merciful smiting Father!* I'd died and shot like a bottle rocket up to Heaven! Those golden gates were wide, wide, wide open! And in the center was Mr. Pink's gigantic, euphoric, awe-inspiring, sparkling body. Yes, Mr. Pink was sparkling like a freaking diamond!

Gee wiz! I just about died again, but just then, Jonas came out of the bathroom. His hair was a bit mussed. His cheeks were flushed. His dark, tan, perfect skin was dark, tan and perfect. So were his muscles. Oh God, he had perfectly and finely defined muscles! I mean, *Hot Diggity Dawg!* Those muscles were perfectly and finely defined, as stated PREVIOUSLY!

"Is that going to be my partner for the shoot?" Mr. Pink asked.

"Yes."

Mr. Pink started unbuttoning his shirt. "I see." He glanced over at me. "You know, it usually isn't until after the first date that I let a girl take my clothes off."

Good Lord! Was he using that line on everybody?

"She's not the one you took your clothes off for, champ," Jonas said, slapping Mr. Pink on the ass with a towel. "I am."

Oh goddess Diana! Shoot that man who's watching you bathe naked! That naughty, naughty boy!

Mr. Pink rolled his eyes. "Let's get this over with."

JONAS WAS ON ALL FOURS, moving his pelvis up and down. A bar was in between his knees, forcing them apart. His bare chest glistened with sweat.

And…And…

Mr. Pink stood above him, his hands on Jonas' hips. His chest sparkled like sunlight on a lake as the sun rises early in the morning —when the only things that exists are you, the gentle ripples in the water, and the quiet, distant chirping of songbirds greeting the day.

Fuck that shit! If I looked much longer, he was gonna blind me! It felt like the backs of my eyes were gonna explode!

"Told you you were gonna thank me," Faythe whispered at my side.

It felt like a wildfire had just spread across my cheeks. No, not my ass cheeks, my face cheeks. You know, the ones between my lips. Not my pussy lips, but my ass lips. I mean my face lips. FUCK! THINKING IS HARD! You know, my fucking mouth okay?

Anyways… "Ugh, thanks."

Faythe clucked her tongue like a chicken leading her little hens across the road. Why did she want to cross? *Oh goodness me!* Were we really gonna GO THERE?

I guess the answer was yes, because we did, but—

"Maggie, are you thinking of something important?" Faythe asked.

"Um, yeah. And you'd never understand it," I said, *because even I can't freaking understand it!*

"Look at how Jonas takes Mr. Pink's abuse," she whispered as Mr. Pink slapped the other man's ass.

"Harder! Slap Harder!" The photographer cried, throwing himself into hysterics.

Mr. Pink frowned.

"Slap the monkey! Slap the haystack! Slap that boy till the cows come home!" The photographer continued.

"Exactly what kind of paper are you writing?" Mr. Pink asked Faythe.

My cheeks went pink. This wasn't for a paper, but for her yaoi fanfic! She wanted live models to study to get the anatomy right. And if I wasn't mistaken, I'd think that right now that Mr. Pink was supposed to be...

"Hump him doggy style! You know, woof woof!" The photographer whimpered, curling his hands up like little paws at his chest and sniffing the air like it was another dog's ass.

"Woof! Woof!" He continued, wagging his butt in Jonas' face.

"Oh, that's rank man!" Jonas barfed his words.

No seriously, he yacked all over the floor.

Looks like Old Faithful is gonna blow!

"Don't clean it. It's raw. Edgy." The photographer declared.

"Alright, what's really going on here?" Mr. Pink bellowed. "There is no way this is for your thesis!"

Just then, some lady brought out a syringe and a twenty inch tube. "Ready for insertion."

Choke while gargling pineapple! That's the longest straw I'd ever freaking seen! What were they drinking in this freaking yaoi fanfic?

Mr. Pink kicked Jonas over and grabbed a cape from the floor. His eyes shot daggers at Faythe and me as he fastened it around his neck and spun around like Dracula. The daggers bounced off me like I was wearing a freaking force field, yo. Or maybe they weren't really daggers at all, but those little primary colored, plastic pirate swords you get in your alcoholic beverages at really classy tiki huts.

"You!" Mr. Pink bellowed, pointing a finger at me.

I wish he'd point something else at me!

No! Wait? *Fucking Lord of Shit!* What else could he possibly point at me? *What was going on with my membrane! (That's another word for brain, right? I mean, those rappers in that one song they sang that one time seemed to use it interchangeably.)*

Anyways, I didn't know what to do. I glanced over at Faythe. She bit her lip. Then, a little light bulb went off over her head. *Literally.* And she grabbed a pen, a conveniently located cardboard sign, and began writing.

"Yeah…" I began. "I…organized…this…photo…shoot…for…myself…not…for…the…paper."

Wait, did I just say that? It was a lie! *Freaking oh no freaky freaky!*

He stepped back, eyes wide. "You did?" He whispered.

Golly Gee! He sounded freaking pained. Had that knowledge made his head explode?

No, his head was still there. Still looking at me.

Wowza! It was so freaking hot in here! That head of his was making me smoke it was so smokin! And not like I had a cigarette, but like my body was so hot that it was steaming, but in a sexy way not in a nasty, moldy fruit way. Not that my nasty, moldy fruit has ever steamed, and by that I mean an actual fruit from the grocery store and not my muffin. *Fuck! TMI, right? CRISIS FUCK!!!* But the 'big point' was if I started to strip, everyone would think I was weird! *Better keep reading off cue cards to confuse them!*

"Yes…" I read as Faythe held up another sign. "I…wanted…to… see…you…sexy…because…I…want…you…so…bad…it…hurts."

Mr. Pink's eyes blazed. "You what?"

I frowned. I actually didn't know what yet. I had to re-read the cue-card before knowing what I'd said because I couldn't remember anything that I ever said when I read out loud.

"What do you want?" Jonas leaped up and body slammed the wall. *Ouch!* He spun around and stuck out his tongue. *Yuck! Boy cooties!* "Why don't you just stomp on my dick, yo?" Jonas asked in a battle cry voice.

"Quick! Stick out your finger, Faythe! I need a cootie immunity shot!"

Jonas and Mr. Pink looked at me like I was a fifty thousand pound bunny rabbit in the chicken coop. *Better than a fox, but fuck! What the fuck is that enormous bunny doing there? How does it even exist, man? I don't know whether I should get the gun, get the camera, or get a listing next to the world's largest ball of yarn!*

Just then, a tumbleweed blew across the picture set, in between Jonas and Mr. Pink. It kind of looked like a ball of yarn.

Oh man, this battle was about to get fucking epic! Extra butter on the popcorn, Papa G!

Ungodly apocalypse fuck! I needed some mind fuel, and fast, because I was *runnin on empty* and the cops were blasting their flashing blue and yellow or white or whatever color behind me!

"I want…" I glanced over at Faythe. She scribbled something else on a sign, and then held it up to me. I had to squint to read it. *Freaking alphabet soup tastes like learning without the rainbow because THE RAINBOW IS A LIE!* Her handwriting was so bad! "To…see…you…wrapped…in…nothing…but…me…"

"Oh, come on babe!" Jonas wailed, kicking the air. He really showed the air who was boss, too. That was one feisty kick. Rawr!

Mr. Pink stepped closer to me. Then closer. Almost as if he was walking towards me…

Oh yeah. Right. He totally was. My bad.

Anyways, when he reached me, he raised his hand as if he were about to touch an irreplaceable ink painting on tissue paper. And really, it was weird. I mean, why would you touch an irreplaceable work of art? Especially one as fragile as ink on tissue paper?

"Look at what you do to me, beautiful girl," he whispered, bringing his hand to his lips. He hadn't touched me. He hadn't even looked like he could stand to look at me, even though it seemed like he couldn't look away.

Oh my goodness gracious!

Before I could say "Oh my goodness gracious" or something even better, he walked out of the room. The last thing I saw before the door closed was his sparkling back disappearing into the perfect darkness of a hallway with no windows and no working lights apparently (someone should really fix that).

5

UGH, HISTORY CLASS. It sucked. I mean, all that stuff happened so long ago. Who cared? It was old, like those Chinese leftovers Faythe had left in the fridge for six months. Both of us were too afraid to touch it because it had started throttling light green ooze, but at some point we knew we had to clean out the fridge, and in case you didn't get my analogy, this institution of freaking "higher learning" needed to clean out its fridge too. I mean, why were they asking questions about Cesar? That salad had been out way too long, and was starting to look freaky, dude.

I slammed my locker on the bright, pink F on my paper. Maybe I could pretend it stood for 'Fabulous'?

"Hi."

I shrieked and fell back. Mr. Pink's face was right next to my locker! Wait, it wasn't just his face! It was actually Mr. Pink! "What are you doing here?"

"I came to see you," he said.

"Oh, well, that's cool. Hey, do you want to go get coffee later—"

"You need to stay away from me, Maggie," he interrupted coolly.

I shook my head. "You came here to tell me to stay away?"

"Yes. I'm bad for you," he whispered. He stepped closer. I bit my bottom lip. "You don't know what you do to me," he whispered.

"What?"

He looked off down the hallway pensively. "I'm leaving. I can't stay. It would have been better if we'd never met."

"Oh, alright," I whispered. *Bummer. Like double bum damn.* But, Lordy, I had the worst caffeine headache ever. I reached down to grab my backpack and looked up to see Mr. Pink running down the hall back at me.

"I can't stay away," he said.

"Okay?"

"But I must. I'm no good for you."

"You mentioned that."

"You have no idea what I'm like," he whispered, pushing me forward in between the edge of the lockers and the drinking fountain. Someone had stuck a wad of gum in the fountain. The pressure built up for a few seconds, and then the gum catapulted off the faucet onto the floor.

At that moment, something exploded inside Mr. Pink too, and he grabbed my arms and slammed me against the wall.

Oh goodness gracious! My stomach swirled. My legs felt weak. Passion bubbled up inside me like a shaken can of soda that bursts everywhere after being opened. Sticky sugary goodness coated my skin like a layer of…spilled soda.

His eyes were smoldering, holding me hostage, binding me to him with the blindingly hot chains of seductive fire. At that moment, I would have gladly jumped to be ravaged on his funeral pyre. My core felt like a shred of ripped silk being caught in his black fist of desire. I whimpered, pressing my soft, tantalizing breasts against his steel chest, wondering if there was a way he could possibly make me feel higher. And yes, I really did feel such things, I am not a liar.

"I'm dangerous, Maggie," he rasped.

"But you just said—"

"I know what I said, and I can't."

He pinned my wrists above my head. "If I was a good man, I'd stay away, but I'm not a good man, Maggie."

His thigh slipped in between my legs, to my lady parts. *Oooh, that feels nice.* My stomach felt as if it were being stretched with agonizing slowness, as if he had a gigantic wad of bubble gum stuck to each hand and was slowly drawing them apart as if playing an accordion.

"Hold on one sec," I said. "If you're this close, I'm gonna pop a mint." *Freaking double wham!* I did not want to hot box him with my garlic breath! I reached into my pocket, popped open the tin, and threw it on my tongue. Ugh, brain freeze! So strong and fresh. "Alright, continue. Wait, you need one too." Didn't want to get hot boxed by *his* garlic breath, either!

His lips parted. I slipped in the winter frost goodness. He bit down, hard, because a man like him doesn't chew, doesn't ever chew, but bites down, hard.

"I'm a bad, bad, man," he hissed. "I've done horrible things. I want to do horrible, horrible things to you. I want to make you mine."

Holy Macaroni! He wanted to make me his? What did that mean?

"You shouldn't be around me."

Huh? Guess I wouldn't learn what he meant, then. "Okay, well, I guess you're leaving?"

He thrust a pile of papers into my hand. "Here."

"What the hell is this?"

"A nondisclosure agreement. I will need you to sign it before I can see you again."

"I thought you just said you can't see me."

He kissed my hand. "That will depend on you."

6

S O I SIGNED THE NONDISCLOSURE agreement. Yeah, I know. Everyone thinks it's dumb. Or at least everyone would if I told them. But I didn't, because I'm double dumb? *Double crap!*

Anyways, I'd already put it in the mail. Wrote out his address in everything. *And I wrote it all out in pink!* Figured he'd like that. But I'd used black ink on my own name to show him that I was my own woman.

Just then, the mailman rang the doorbell and personally handed me a letter from Mr. Pink. *But ungodly shit man!* I was in a dorm room and this was totally out of his way. That's what I call service!

Anyways, I opened it.

Inside was a note that said: "See you at six," and the keys to the most expensive and luxurious car in the world: a Merabies.

"WHAT THE HELL IS THIS?" I screamed when I saw Mr. Pink.

"Excuse me?"

"What. The. Fuck." I yelled, hurling the keys at him. "These are for a Merabies! A Mer-Ray-Bees! All those fancy-pants cars have all these super expensive custom parts that you have to order specially and are freaking impossible to find!"

Mr. Pink's jaw quirked (God that sounds painful). "You drive around a piece of trash!"

"It's not a piece of trash!" I told him. Then, a much more puzzling thought popped into my brain. "Wait, you've never seen my car. How do you know what it looks like?"

"Of course I've seen your car," Mr. Pink told me. "I have you under 24-hour satellite surveillance."

"Um, what?"

"And I have hidden webcams in your room."

"What?"

"And a tracker implanted into you cell phone!"

"WHAT?"

"And one in your brain."

"WHAT THE FUCK?"

"Anyways, your car is unsafe and unacceptable. I bought one that was safer and more suitable for a lady of your stature."

"No! This is where I put my foot down!" I yelled, putting my foot down. "I am a car mechanic. I know it seems unlikely, especially if you asked me really specific, or even really general, questions about cars, because I wouldn't be able to answer them, but that 'unsafe and unacceptable' car just happens to be my body and soul!"

Mr. Pink flinched.

"Look, a car isn't just a car to me! It is a baby. *My baby!* Like, it came out from my mind womb. *My mind womb!* That car you hate so much? I made that from scratch. I found it part by part and put it together with a hammer and duct tape. Some welding equipment too, but you'd be surprised what you can make with duct tape. I have a friend who made a really cool wallet out of duct tape. But that doesn't matter!" I put my hand on his shoulder. "That car is a part of me, and if you can't learn to accept it, then there is no way you could ever accept me."

"Does that piece of junk really mean that much to you?" He asked.

"I don't know. Does your 'piece of junk' mean that much to you?"

"Touché, Miss Sterling," he whispered with a smile. "I'm sorry you found my gift unsatisfactory."

"It's okay. Not every gift can be a winner. Besides, aren't you gonna take me out to dinner?"

His lips quirked up. "How presumptuous of you."

"Well, it's six and I'm fucking hungry. If you're not taking me out, I'm ordering pizza."

"No. No. I want you. All of you. *Tonight.* Let's go eat."

Damn! He sometimes talked with a ton of pauses! And they were really freaking awkward too! But that would be mean to bring up, right? Yeah, it would be. "Okay, we can go, but we're taking my car."

"Alright," he smiled.

"You don't mind riding shotgun, do you?" I asked.

"Not if you're the one behind the wheel."

"I CAN'T BELIEVE YOU drive a freaking Volva!" Mr. Pink said.

"Volvas are great cars. They rarely break down. Besides, they're what all the super hunks in teenage romance novels drive." For some reason, even though I said that, I thought that he did, so I responded to myself, but I thought it was him. "You're not a teenage romance—wait, how do you know what guys in those books drive?"

He smiled. "All that I'm saying is that I trust your judgment."

I nodded. "Good." I trusted my judgment too!

"If you think this hunk of junk is better than that Merabies in the parking lot, then I trust your judgment."

"Really?"

"Yes.

Those were really touching words, but they didn't really mean much when the car broke down fifteen minutes later on the highway.

I threw my head onto the steering wheel. The horn blared out my "Shit!" (I'll just let you think about that totally unintended image for a second.)

I glanced over at Mr. Pink. "Don't you dare say anything!"

"Wouldn't dream of it."

"Really?" I asked.

"Yes. I trust your tastes, remember?"

"Oh, now you're just making fun of me."

"No I'm not. If this is the car you chose, and this is the one you really like, well, there isn't much I can say about it, is there? I trust your tastes, Maggie." He put his hands under my chin, tilting up my head. His face was outlined in moonlight. That strong, severe jaw, the high angle of his cheekbones, those eyes that smoldered, were all focused on me as if I were the only thing in this world that existed to him.

"Alright. So I destroyed dinner." I moaned.

"No, you haven't."

"What do you mean? There is no way we are gonna get there in time."

"I can call my driver—"

"No, I can't leave my baby out here all alone and vulnerable!"

He glanced at the car, as if he thought it was a hunk of junk. "What?"

"Someone might steal it! Someone might hit it! I can't leave it out here. I'm sorry. You can go. You should go."

He paused. "You actually think someone is going to try to steal this thing?"

"You don't understand how much she means to me!" I shrieked.

He sighed. "Do you really think I'm the kind of guy who would just leave you out here, alone, by the side of the road?"

"Well…"

"Stop," he whispered. "If that's really your answer, I don't want to hear it."

Sweet Mary and Joseph and Abraham and Isaiah! He was so freaking romantic! "It's just that it's your favorite restaurant. You were looking forward to going," I told him.

"Were you looking forward to it, too?"

"Well, duh."

"Duh," his lips curled up. "It is too bad that we can't go, but that doesn't mean our dinner is ruined."

"What do you mean?"

"We'll just have to bring them to us."

"What?"

He took out his mePhone and started dialing.

"Wait, what are you doing?"

"Bringing dinner," he whispered, and then placed one of his fingers over my lips. "Don? Yes. Bring our food in." He glanced over at me. "What would you like?"

"Um, I don't know. I guess whatever."

"Really? Adventurous girl," he whispered admirably. I didn't like the way he said 'adventurous,' but I couldn't really take it back since he seemed to like it.

"I'd like to order the menu."

Ooohhh, classy pants! *Which are so much classier than fancy pants!*

He hung up. "It should be here in about fifteen minutes."

"Yay. So hungry I could eat a horse!"

He began to pout. I suddenly remembered the unicorn headed secretary. "I mean…a house. Or a hose. I mean, you could just stick a house through a wood chopper and I'd suck it out of a hose." There. That sounded tasty.

Not.

But in the end it didn't matter, because his expression lightened.

Then it darkened again. From sexy hotness, not anger. "So Maggie," he rasped. "What do you think of a man that orders the menu?"

"Honestly?" I shifted on my feet.

"Yes. Honestly."

"Well, I hope he'll share."

Mr. Pink laughed. "Oh, your rapier wit!" He glanced down with a puzzled expression. "Good Lord! Is that a nickel and a dime I see? I can understand leaving a penny behind, but a nickel and a dime! What were they thinking?"

Just then, my blood went cold.

No. Oh God no!

"Stop. Leave them alone!" I wailed.

Mr. Pink sighed. "I'm a businessman, Miss Sterling. I can't leave money lying on the ground. It's against my entrepreneurial spirit." He bent over.

No! He was getting closer to them! I couldn't take it! "God Damn! I hate nickels and dimes! Get those away!"

He looked up at me. "Why?"

"Because they just don't make sense," I explained.

He frowned. "What do you mean?"

"I mean, look at this," I shook as I picked up his nickel and his dime and held them in my hand. *Damn, these things gave me the willies!* "Alright. Which one is bigger?" I asked.

"The nickel," he answered.

"Right, now, which one is worth more?"

"The dime."

I balled up my fist and threw them at him. "Exactly!"

"I don't get it."

"Why isn't the one that's bigger worth more?"

He paused. "You know what? I don't actually know."

"I know you don't know," I whispered, looking to the night sky, trying to find comfort in the blinking, lonely stars, shining so brightly for someone, anyone, yet finding no one in the night sky but those other stars they can never reach. "It took me three years to accept this. No, I still haven't accepted it. It's too ridiculous to accept. It took me years to even acknowledge this was how things were. That society could deem this true and correct, even though it made no sense. That the world would not listen to my arguments, regardless of how thoughtful they were, because this lie had already become convention. In the end, they didn't care that it made no sense that nickels were larger than dimes but worth less. They didn't care!"

My chest rose, my cheeks were flushed. He put his hand on the side of my face.

"No, don't comfort me!" I cried, slapping his hand away. He moaned as I struck him. I continued: "It hurts me, deeply, agonizingly, to my core, to know that I must accept things in this world that I know in my heart are wrong just because society demands it. When I realized that yes, nickels were in fact worth less than dimes even though they were bigger, a little part of my innocence died that day."

I picked them up. They were in the mud. I rubbed my thumb over some dead president's head that no one remembered because *hot damn!* he was fucking old! "I mean, a dime is even smaller than a penny. Seriously, what the fuck?"

He bent down and covered my trembling, mud-coated hands with his own.

I choked up, but I couldn't let the soreness in my throat stop me from continuing. I had to keep going! I had to! "You know that saying 'nickel and dime' you? Well, what that really means is that person wants to reveal to you how ugly and nonsensical the world is, and how powerless you are to change any of it! They keep us ignorant and impotent and depressed! That is how they control us!"

"I see," he murmured.

"Are you making fun of me?"

"No, I just didn't realize how deep you were. I never thought about it that way before. It just makes me wonder if any other economic theories are lies. Like, if you can't have infinite growth on a finite planet."

"No, you can," I reasoned. "Because you can always think up new stuff to do, and your head space is infinite."

"Damn, you're smart. I wasn't expecting you to be such a thrilling conversationalist. Are you sure you're not a philosophy major?"

"No. I'm undecided," I said.

"I thought you were a senior?"

"I am credit wise, but I can never stay in one place long enough, you know? I mean, except P-Town, because I've lived here all my life. But I mean, like, in school. Each time I learn about a subject I want to learn about the next. I don't think I'll ever be able to master every academic discipline in my lifetime."

"I think you can," Mr. Pink murmured softly, because really, there's no other way to murmur. "I think you can do anything you put your mind to."

"Well, except make a running car, apparently."

"Oh, you can do that too," he said. "You just need to find someone to supply the right parts. So, how about you stick your hand down my pants?"

Before I could stick my hand down his pants to pull out whatever spare part he offered, the food came. Like, a helicopter hovered right over us and caused a massive traffic accident, but it was on the other side of the turnpike so whatever. Sirens started blaring and Mr. Pink and I had to yell to each other to communicate. It was hard to hear him, honestly. Like, I couldn't tell what he said. And I didn't understand why he kept gesturing to his pants. I already had my napkin in my lap!

Mr. Pink watched me eat, which was a mistake on his part, because I ended up eating the entire menu.

"What do you think of a girl that eats the menu after you order it?" I asked him.

He cupped my cheek. "I think she's the most one-of-a-kind-gal in the world."

Holy hot dogs! I'm so fucking tired of hot dog phrases by now that I think I'm gonna puke the next time I see a hot dog!

7

THE NEXT DAY, TWO meatheads in suspicious looking business suits escorted me to a limo parked outside my dorm room. Inside was Mr. Pink.

"There's something I haven't told you yet," he said, filling up a glass of champagne for me.

Oh my! My hand shook as I accepted it, and I spilled it all over us.

"I'm so sorry!" I exclaimed in a girlie tone.

"That's alright. It's my fault."

"No, really. I'm such a klutz—"

"No! It's my fault!" He screamed, and then hurled the champagne bottle against the car door.

"Oh no," I said.

Mr. Pink balled up his fists and started hammering his temples with them. "I'm sorry for that too. It's just what you do to me, Miss Sterling. I can't control myself any longer."

Oh sweet merciful Mary!

He looked up at me, his dark eyes filled with a longing all women yearn to see just once in their lives—the kind of longing that consumes you, frightens you, possesses you…

"I want to fuck you, Miss Sterling," he said.

"What?" For a second I thought he'd just said he wanted to fuck me!

"I said I want to fuck you," he repeated.

Alright. I guess he really did say that.

Mr. Pink explained the situation further: "I want to spread apart your legs and ram my cock inside you. I want to rut you like a raging bull. I want to imprint my brand deep inside your womb."

Oh swanky panky. My womb responded, swimming up to my throat. Wait, that's gross. I mean, my heart began beating really fast. My womb stayed where it was. *Down girl! What the fuck?*

"So you want to make love to me," I whispered.

He laughed—low and grim, a darkly musical sound. "I don't make love, sweetheart. I hump. Hard."

Hump hard? *Oh gees!*

"I trust you read the nondisclosure agreement," he said.

"Uh, yeah," I lied. I totally hadn't read it. I didn't think I needed to. I mean, I wasn't supposed to disclose anything, right? Well, the best way to not disclose something was to not know anything about it in the first place. That was my thought. But suddenly I didn't want to tell him that.

"So you know what I want to do to you, or at least a little bit of it," he rasped.

God, the veins in his forehead were pulsating really freaking hard! Was he constipated? How long had he been stuck out here in his limo, waiting for me to come out? "Dude, lets get out of here!"

He glanced up, taking a deep breath. "So glad you said that. My thoughts exactly. Driver, to my underground lair."

Underground lair? *What the fuck!* Was that where he made his evil hot dogs?

The car sped into the night. I know I said it was daytime before, at the beginning of this chapter, like right before I got in the car, but right now it's nighttime. It took him for-fucking-ever to pour that champagne!

Beethoven serenaded us. His piano playing, that is. Actually, some guy no one knows was playing Beethoven, not Beethoven himself. I mean, Beethoven was dead before people could record shit, and I do mean *shit*.

"Let's discuss a few things before we go any further," Mr. Pink drawled.

A chill crept over my skin as he spoke, as if his breath was made of dry ice. "Okay."

"The hard limits, I think," he whispered, brushing his finger over my thigh. "The things you absolutely will not do, under any circumstances."

My throat felt tight. My insides seemed to be churning with need. But what did I need, exactly? His finger on my leg made me need things, like his touch, but the more he touched me the more I needed! What the fuck? FUCK!

"My hard limits are quite simple," he purred. "No bowling on hump night. No taking out the trash. No scaphism. No nipple clamps."

Well, that all sounded pretty okay. Who liked to bowl on hump night? Too many freaking people out, gyrating their hips to that crappy pop crap they always played at the ally. And take out the trash? Who would want to do that? And who fucking knew what scaphism was anyway? I didn't want to do shit I didn't know. And nipple clamps…

WAIT? WHAT THE FUCK? NIPPLE CLAMPS? WERE THOSE WHAT I THOUGHT THEY WERE? DID THEY GO WHERE IT SOUNDED LIKE THEY WENT?

"Soft limits, the things we can negotiate," he continued. "Pony play. Bondage. Natello. Feathers. St. Albert. Butt plugs."

Holy moley macaroni! Did he just say *butt plugs*? BUTT PLUGS? FOR FUCKING REAL?

I tried to sit up to tell the driver to STOP THE FUCKING CAR NOW!!!! But Mr. Pink held me down.

"No need to be so eager, sweetheart. We have the entire night ahead of us."

An entire night of nipple clamps and butt plugs? I preferred evil hot dogs!

"You haven't let me finish," he murmured, breathless. "Bedtime stories. And…snuggling."

Tension left my shoulders. "Snuggling?"

"Yes. Snuggling. Oh, we're here," he said as the car zoomed down a secret under ground passage way beneath Pink Towers.

Magical Manimal!

"We're almost there," he whispered, eyes gleaming. "My secret, underground lair. And…my dungeon."

8

Part 1 of the Interior Goddess' monologue

THE HALLWAY WAS ALMOST completely dark. Green strands of silk hung from the ceiling, like seaweed blowing in the infinite silence of the ocean. I was submerged forcefully. My ears started ringing, and the ancient starfish twinkling in the distance looked like stars on the horizon.

And then, I saw a vision.

A woman, slowly moving her hands as if time were sifting through her fingers like sand. She was spinning moonlight at her spinning wheel. And it was as if time and space were simplified into a microscopic point within the infinite space of the universe, and yet, that one pinprick upon eternity was as large as the space that contained it, until both the thing that contained everything and the thing that conveyed nothing were one and the same.

This is what poets whisper, as they find solace with one another in the shadows of a crowded street, pressing their lips to the soft, sensitive surface of skin beneath your ear; This is what they whisper, when they find themselves alone as the sounds of eternity are played upon the heart inside the cage of their chests, longing to be broken free; The sound of their voice moves with that song that all of us were born singing, but none of us remember when we are dying. All we can hope for is to shut our eyes and sink back into the amoeba of consciousness.

Linger, sweet heart. And whimper as darkness closes around you; as eternity closes around you; as you scream out for another, another, another, always; as you scream until your soul weeps; as you scream until comfort is a scream, and the roughness of your throat is a kiss, and as you surrender yourself to the gods that have kept you prisoner, for even the touch of your captors feels beautiful after spending so much time alone.

9

I WALKED DOWN THE HALLWAY. Fuck! I felt so weird for some reason. I glanced over at Sir. Hotness Pink. *Oh yeah, he knows how to work it.*

Wait! *Jesus and Holy St. Mother Teresa of Guacamole!* I was like almost practically going somewhere I didn't know...which would make sense since I'd never been here before....but it felt like something...something...FUCK!

Alright. Calm down. Maggie. Calm the fuck down and try to remember what it was you were supposed to remember. There was something you weren't supposed to know.

Golly gee! Where were these voices coming from? Why was my Interior Goddess rearing her bloody head? Why did she demand attention? And why did she speak so freaking weird? And who the fuck was she anyway?

Wait a moment before you shit! (*Yes, seriously, wait a moment. You're probably WTF-ing so hard right now that you don't even think this is funny! I mean, you're just trying to fucking figure out what the FUCK is going on! Don't worry. Thinking about it won't help you understand. In fact, pretty much fucking nothing you can do will help you understand because EVEN I DON'T KNOW WHAT THE FUCK IS GOING ON and I, Faythe Freaking America, am the one writing this shit).*

While I thought things like this (and yeah, it was like pulling out your hair until all that's left are scabs on your skull), Mr. Pink was staring at me like something had just gone seriously wrong.

And I guess something had.

Depending on your definition of 'wrong.'

And you definition of 'something.'

"Miss Sterling," he said.

"Yes?"

"The thing that I am about to show you I have never shown anyone, except for the tens other women I have taken as lovers to perfect the carnal arts."

"Carnal arts? Have you, like, eaten dogs or something with carnies?"

Mr. Pink looked at me like I'd just slapped him, and then decided to continue on as if I'd said nothing. "I trust you've thought long and hard about what you read in the nondisclosure agreement."

"Um, sure." *Did I read that bitch?* No, I just gave her a tattoo (i.e. signed my name along her tramp stamp, i.e. the little line where your signature goes on the bottom of legal forms).

He took in a deep breath. "And you're alright with all of it?"

I suddenly felt like I should tell him that I hadn't read it, but I didn't, because that would give him the edge in our business agreement because he would know something that I didn't t know…

but *double scooped ice cream crap!* I didn't know what things I was supposed to know! So didn't that already give him the upper hand? *Low-five because you don't deserve high-five crap!* So before I even came up with a game plan, he already had the upper hand! And he was a lot taller than me! So when he stuck his hand in the air for the 'high-five' and I couldn't reach it everyone would laugh! And…

Wait! He doesn't know! Not yet! "Of course. I know everything." I grabbed his pink tie and yanked on it, bringing him down to my level so that our noses touched. "And now that I know everything, I am going to use it to control you."

His eyes fluttered shut. He shuddered in the palm of my hand, like the quivering leaf of a Japanese Oak, before it follows the subtle, downward slope of its languid branches in its fatalistic descent towards decomposition and rebirth.

He moved his cheek, slowly, along my palm. He'd shaved before he met me. I could still smell the aftershave, of periwinkles and peppermint. Then, his bottom lip brushed against my palm.

He flicked his tongue against it. I could feel it, a damp, dangerous promise, seeping into my skin. Seeping through my membrane into my blood. Because nothing is sexier than thinking of someone's germs penetrating the protective layer of your body. *Super sunbathing llama piranha crap!*

I moaned. A small sound in the back of my throat.

Oh Groovy Shit! My tonsils are tingling!

His lips opened.

My finger slipped in, at first because I wondered if his tonsils were having sympathy tingles for mine. But before I could relieve his itch, he caressed my finger with his tongue.

*Mmmm…*He'd suckled raw garlic before he'd picked me up.

Mayhap he thought I was a vampire. Mayhap I was, and tonight, he was going to be my victim. Mayhap speaking in pretend Middle English made me sound smart, and mayhap it didn't.

"I am ready to show you my dungeon," he whispered, grabbing my wrist, slamming me into the wall. His knee slipped in between my legs. I arched my hips against it. It being his legs, not his cock, because I was a virgin, not a nasty, disgusting, filthy, whore-bag like my *bff-forever* Faythe!

He gave me the reach around.

Oh, dirty grandpa's wearing only his suspenders again crap!

I was upset, though, when he grabbed the doorknob that had apparently been digging into my back for the past twenty seconds instead of my ass.

"You know what this means, Miss Sterling," he whispered.

"Uh, look. I love garlic as much as the next person, but don't put your mouth on my nose, okay? Moist garlic is just rank, dude."

"This means," he continued, stepping back, eyes black because he was just such a freaking dark dangerous derringer-wielding debonair! "I'm about to turn you into liquid gold."

I gasped as he leaned forward and we fell into the room.

The lights flickered on.

I saw what was around me.

In the most secret part of his secret lair. In his *dungeon*.

And I screamed.

10

EVERYTHING WAS PINK. Freaking everything. *Holy god-smacked shit! I'm gonna have to gargle salt water for a freaking week!* A pink, heart-shaped bed lay in the center of the room. A pink canopy stretched from the ceiling. No, canopy wasn't the right word. It was like an Arabian princess' bed.

Hell yeah! Where's the magic carpet Aladdin?

The ceiling sparkled like a freaking pink diamond! No wait! It WAS a pink diamond! HOLY FUCK? "Is that one diamond?"

"Yes."

"No shit! I mean, total shit! I mean, you've blown the shit out of my mind! Isn't that like the world's biggest diamond?"

Mr. Pink grinned and his dick gave his hand a high-five through his pants! *Oh sweet Susan!* "I'm the owner of many of the biggest things in the world." He said, tone as cocky as his cock.

"Oh my!"

"Oh my what, babe?"

"Are those My Lil Horsies? No fucking way! I used to play with these when I was a little girl."

Mr. Pink tilted his head. "Why did you stop?"

"I don't know. Turned 10. I mean, it's not like you can play with My Lil Horsies for forever."

"Why not?" Mr. Pink demanded, his cheeks flushed.

"Well…" My cheeks flushed too.

"Why can't you do what you want when you're a grown man?" He bellowed, slamming his fist into the pink yarn carpet on the floor. "Why can't you play with My Lil Horsies when you're the most fucking successful billionaire on the planet? Why not? I have all the fucking money in the entire world! I should be able to do what I want!"

"Dude," I said. "That is so fucking right. Why can't billionaires play with Horsies? Fuck!"

His nostrils flared as his cheeks flushed again! Mine flushed too, right after his did! And we began a flushing war, one person's cheeks flushing, and then the others, until both our faces were so red that steam was coming out the top like little red teapots!

"You're fucking right," Mr. Pink said. He grabbed me and slammed me against the bedpost. The ridge of the post rubbed right against my ass. I moaned and pushed into it. "I'm so glad you understand. Fuck! You don't know how hard it is to control myself around you, Miss Sterling."

He pushed me down onto the bed, his hands gripping my shoulders so tight that already I could feel them bruise.

"Hey dude! That fucking hurts!" I yelled, slamming my fist into his neck. "Oh shit! Way too hard! Sorry!"

Mr. Pink moaned and arched his back. "Again!"

"What?" I frowned.

"Do it again! Fuck! Again! Harder!"

"What the hell is wrong, dude? Do you like have Tourette's or something?"

"The ball gag is in the end table next to the bed."

"Ball gag?"

He licked his lips, looking down at me with untamed eagerness, as if he were 16 years old and having sex for the first time on his girlfriend's couch while her parents were at church. "You're mad that I used a pet name, aren't you, baby? There, I did it again," he whispered, leaning forward. "I'm such a bad boy. Tell me how bad I am and spank me!"

"FUCK!" I yelled. This dude was messed up!

I pushed him and he fell back on the bed. "That's right!" He yelled, spreading his legs. He pulled down his pants. "Please, Mistress Sterling. Pick up the riding crop by the door and punish your bad little boy! Turn my ass cheeks fifty shades of pink!"

11

.

M Y CHEEKS TURNED FIFTY shades of pink. (My face cheeks. Not my ass cheeks.) "What?" I whispered, backing up. Mr. Pink was still on the bed. Fucking humping the bed. *That's right. He doesn't make love. He just humps hard. And apparently he must need to reupholster his furniture all the freaking time!*

Oh lordy me!

"Remember the hard limits." He licked his lips. "And no bowling on hump night, Mistress Sterling. The only strikes you're gonna get are coming from me."

"What the freaking big-will(ow)y-style-fuck is going on here?" I looked up. "Is that a freaking disco light?"

"I want the night to sparkle!" Mr. Pink declared, jumping on the bed and clapping his hands. "There's a dildo in the bedside drawer, too. Want to ravage my ass?"

There are some words that are repeated again and again and again in Romance novels.

Seduction is a boring example. *Surrender* is a little sexier, but still pretty damn tame. And then there are the words that start with the letter right before S. Like *racecar* (which is almost never used in Romance novels), and *rumble* (which totally should be used in romance novels more. Let's rumble in the bed sheets!)

And *ravage*.

Oh yes, ravage *is* quite a word. First, because it is a word, and second, because it is a *saucy* word. A word full of ingredients of meaning. Like fucking. Taking. Conquering. Penis shoving into the vagina super hardcore, until he squirts his man sauce into her apple pie, aka her baby making nightmare abyss of HELL!

But that doesn't matter. The point is, *ravage* is what *dicks* do to *woman swamp holes*.

Ravage is *not* what *a piece of plastic* does to a *billionaire's ass*.

"Oh ungodly holy fire!" I whimpered.

Mr. Pink frowned. Sat. Pulled up his pants. "Miss Sterling, I am going to ask you a question, and I want you to answer it honestly."

"Alright. Think I can do that."

"No, you do not think you can do it, you will do it."

"That too."

"Miss Sterling," he punctuated each syllable like a Shakespearean actor, so spit was flying everywhere. I was glad his eight foot Rainbow Brilliant doll had the front seat and not me. "Did you read the nondisclosure agreement?"

Hot diggity do-dad (ha-ha! You thought I was gonna say Hot DOG! Psych!) *Freaky totally freaky-freaky-in-the-room-without-a-peeky fuck!* "Uh…I didn't. I mean, I was planning on…not reading it. But I was going to…think about what could be in it."

"What?" Mr. Pink gasped. He hadn't finished his word before he started gasping, so he ended up choking and I gave him the Heimlich maneuver to save his life. Then, we got back in our positions, each of us on either side the #1 enemy of weatherman everywhere, our mediator Rainbow Brilliant.

"Look. It was like long and stuff. Not quite as long as my history book, but fuck, I didn't read that either!"

"You should never sign something before you read it! Hell, before you get your lawyer's opinion on it!"

"Lawyer?" I laughed. "Fuck! I'm like, in my early twenties or something." No idea how old I really was, because I hadn't really planned that far ahead when I started this story. "How many people in their twenties have a fucking lawyer?"

"I do!"

"You're not in your twenties. You're like in your eighties and just got plastic surgery to look like you were in your twenties."

"WHAT?" Mr. Pink raged.

"You have a lot of shit for a twenty year old."

"I have a lot of shit," Mr. Pink rasped, "because I like my own things. I have a lot of shit because I've worked harder than everyone else to gain my position, so that no one can ever tell me what I want and do not want, what I can do and can't do, again. That's right, mommy!" He screamed, pointing an accusatory finger towards the sea of diamonds in the sky. "It is NOT my bedtime yet!"

"Wow," I whispered, my lips glistening with sweat. My sweat probably made my lips look like diamonds. Or maybe I should have said spittle, because why *the flying fuck face-fuck* would my lips be sweating at all, let alone that much? But then again, both are pretty fucking disgusting, so it probably would have been better if I hadn't said anything at all.

Mr. Pink shook his head back and forth, like he was looking both ways before crossing the street. *Watch out for sk8 boarding ruffians, yo!* "Now, are you honestly telling me that you did absolutely no research on Loving Female Authority?"

"Huh?"

Mr. Pink rolled his eyes. "Alright. Do you know anything at all about femdoms?"

"Fem? Dom? Is that like a fermented dome banana from Iowa or something?"

"What the *fuck* are you talking about?"

I squinted at him. *Face-palm masterful fuck!* Faythe wasn't here to give me cue card notes! If only she were here to tell me what to say! Then Mr. Pink might like me!

Mr. Pink sighed and started to head bang as if he were listening to Striper. *Fuck! Calm the tiger, manisupial! (That's a man marsupial, in case that wasn't clear.) You're gonna freaking get whiplash!*

"Do you even know anything about sex?" It sounded like he was talking through a fan because he was still head banging like a motherfucker.

"No. I'm still a virgin."

Mr. Pink spun around. "What?"

"Never 'done the nasty'."

"What?"

"Never been porked." *Snort snort!*

"WHAT?"

"Never been boned, man."

He grabbed my shoulders and shook me, shook me so hard, as if I were salt and pepper and he had some foul meat that was in desperate need of seasoning to cover up the rancid taste. "You're untouched?"

"Come on, dude! I bathe myself! I'll go a week or a month sometimes without busting out the soap bar, if ya know what I mean, but come on, 21 years is a little too much, don't you think?" Oh, so that's how old I was!

He picked me up and threw me down on my back. "No! No! You can't be a virgin."

"Huh?"

He bit his fist and looked around all paranoid, like a fish that was afraid it would be out of water. (Fishes do not like to play 'Marco Polo', especially when they are the only fish in the swimming pool.) "No. I must save you. I must..." His fingers dug into my shoulders. "I must rid you of your hymen!"

"My hymen!" *Oh goodness me!*

"Yes. That foul cage that traps your blissful woman fruit!"

"Woman fruit? What does it taste like?" *Hey! I told you there was a reason I brought up bananas earlier! That's a bull's-eye for the bull with a little circle around its eye! Ride me, rodeo clown! (Cowboys are so passé.)*

"Yes. I can't feast upon it until your body is ready for me."

I looked at him. Really looked. Like, really hard and super close. Maybe I shouldn't have looked so close. I mean, he was like the hottest guy in the world, right? Well, even the hottest guy in the world has a few flaws, and I was seeing them since we were in low lighting and our faces were super close. Like, he had a few blackheads on his nose and one of his eyelids closed a little further over his eye than the other eyelid. *Oh I can't believe it's* not *not-buttery fuck!* I mean, FUCK! I felt like such a bitch for bringing it up, but it was true.

And then, a tear started to bud in my eye like a budding rose. Luckily, there are such things as thornless roses, because holy shit, it would have hurt super bad for a rose to be growing inside my eyeball.

Sniff! Sniff! Does it smell like Old Sauce in here? Fuck, get some anal bleach, man!

"I can't!" I cried, throwing myself on the bed and dramatically pressing the back of my wrist to my forehead. Then, I cried again, throwing myself over a pink chair he had next to his vanity. Then I cried, thrice, and belly flopped onto the floor at his feet.

"Why not?" Mr. Pink cried. He couldn't stand anymore because his need for me was so great, so he decided to crush my ribs by slapping his junk on my face. And no, I'm not talking about his cock junk, I'm talking about his My lil Horsie parts, and they weren't erotic! A stampede of pastel rainbow colored horsies leaped from the shelf he'd shipwrecked himself on (doesn't that sound more dramatic than 'threw himself on'?).

I rolled on the floor, groaning.

Mr. Pink saw his misplaced horsie friends and collapsed. "Why can't you let me hump you dry?"

"Dry? Dude, don't hump your laundry!" What would a sassy middle-aged maid think? Well, unless he planned to hang up his wet clothes on his massive dick stick.

Mr. Pink crouched over me, like a fallen angel crouching over a sinner who had died before the fallen angel could save the sinner's soul, thereby condemning both himself (because he failed his one chance to regain God's favor) and the sinner (for failing to be saved) to an eternity in Hell.

But luckily that dramatic fate wasn't in the cards for either of us.

Even though my face flushed right again, which must be a world record for face-flushing or something, I wasn't dead. And Mr. Pink was no angel.

Not a dark man like him. With such a tight, white ass that he wanted me to turn fifty shades of pink.

Oh my double craps!

I looked away. Oh, I wasn't worthy! I would never be! "I can't let you hump me! I'm not pretty enough."

"Miss Sterling, right now you could be the ugliest woman on the planet and I'd still want to fuck you because I have a raging boner."

I looked at him and wailed. "WAAAA! YOU THINK I'M FAT!"

"What? When did I say that?"

"You'd fuck me even if I was the ugliest girl!"

"Well, yes, but that's because I respect your beautiful mind! And I seriously want to fuck that sweet, tight cunt!"

I pushed him away. Mr. Pink wasn't next to me when I started to push, so I had to get up to push him, then I got back down on the floor.

"Look, why would a delicate skunkweed like you think that you're ugly?" He asked.

Skunkweed? Damn his honeyed tongue! But I was not some butterfly that would blindly bind herself to any man who offered me sugar! "I'm just not hot and I know it, alright?" I mean, did I really have to relay my horrible experience at that 'Hot or Not' website?

"Have you ever looked in a mirror?" Mr. Pink rasped.

My blood responded to his husky, sexy, manly tone by scrubbing up and down like a dish woman's washrag. I glanced at a rhinestone studded mirror in the corner and started to think about what I looked like.

I wasn't hideous. Alright, I looked pretty good, in that innocent girl cute kind of way. In that super model runway kind of way. In that way that every girl on the planet wants to look kind of way. But shit like that doesn't mean shit if you have a Mary Sue complex!

"Look, I don't understand why I think I'm so ugly or unattractive. It's almost like I'm a paper-thin character in a thinly plotted novel. It's like, some author wanted to give me a problem but didn't actually want to give me one so they gave me a fake problem, and all it does is make me look even more perfect than I already am! Because no one will love me unless I'm perfect! I have to be a drop-dead-gorgeous yet curiously-quirky virgin or else I won't be worthy of being a manwhore stalker's sex toy! And I can't have interesting thoughts or else I'll wonder why I'm wasting away my life waiting for that said, manipulative, creepy daddy-figure to realize that he wants me to be his trophy wife instead of doing something that I WANT TO DO!"

"So, you agree you're cute, right?" Mr. Pink asked.

"Yes. But that still doesn't explain why you like me."

He grinned. "You want to know?"

"Yeah. I do."

"Really?"

"Really!"

He nodded. "It's the way you bite your lip," he said. "No other girl on the face of this earth bites her lip in that way."

"Um, what?"

"I can read fifty thousand things into that single lip bite."

Was he on something? "Like what?"

"Like, that you want me. Like, that you want me to bite it."

He leaned forward and took it between his lips, softly, far more softly than I did. Slowly, his tongue ran over it

"And when I kiss that lip that has been so vigorously gnawed on, it's rough, rough as sandpaper, such an erotic contrast to your smooth, silky tongue," he said.

My cunt clenched. Did he just make sand paper—sand paper on a girl's—no, on MY lips—sound sexy?

"With lips like sandpaper, how can you possibly stay away from me?" I asked.

It sounded ridiculous, but Mr. Pink was seriously hardcore. "How can I is right. You could polish wood with those lips."

"Polish wood? Now that's just ridiculous."

"I wasn't talking about wood from trees, sweetheart."

I took a step back. "What wood isn't from trees?"

He grinned at me, and my gaze followed his, to the tepee in his trousers.

My heart stopped.

"I think you finally got it," he said. "How would you like to polish my wood, sweetheart?"

My throat closed, as if it was already gagged by his...'wood.'

"I can handle a little bit of pain from you. You can rock me like Woodley tha Wood-Pecker."

12

More from the Interior Goddess...Ugh...

M AGGIE'S VOICE ECHOES somewhere in the distance: *Oh sweet Hannah Savannah! But before her hardcore bossy tones can be heard from all over the valley, another voice calls out!*

Hot Dogs: Hey, don't forget about us! You used to make a hot dog reference like three times every freaking paragraph! Now you're all 'shit' and 'fuck' and 'crap.' Aren't you worried about how all the children who read this book are going to react to your potty mouth?

Interior Goddess: Shut up you stupid Hot Dogs! I know your real plan! You're trying to find the evil hot dog factory so you can inject yourselves with rabies so you can bite everyone who dares to eat another hot dog and turn them into zombie hot dogs!

Hot Dogs: Ho! How did you find out our master plan?

Interior Goddess: I knew you hot dogs were up to something! With all those "diggitys" and getting it on with corn!

Hot Dogs: I'd like some mustard on that FUCK! Wait! No, it doesn't matter! Because Maggie doesn't know how to talk to her

Interior Goddess!

Interior Goddess: Wait! NOOO!!!!!

Hot Dogs: *laugh as smoke rises from the forests of the night* Yes! Soon the world will be nothing but hot dogs! And then the burritos and the hamburgers, which look down on us now, will know the true taste of vengeance! Which is, by the way, the taste of pureed broccoli!

Interior Goddess: *screams as her golden form is swallowed by the darkness of hell*

Scene: Hot dogs get out of bed, take a catsup bath and put on their mustard aftershave, pet their dog-pickle, go their closet, put on their buns like winter coats, and zip them up.

And when Billy ordered a hot dog from his favorite hot dog stand in the middle of San Francisco, he didn't suspect a thing.

-Fin

13

"LIKE A WOODPECKER? I mean that woodpecker? The hahaha one?" I asked super loud. Mr. Pink nodded his head. With a flick of his wrist, he simultaneously unzipped his belt and unfastened his zipper, and while that doesn't sound possible I just want to reiterate that a lot of *crazy fucking shit* goes down when Mr. Pink flicks his manly wrists.

Mr. Pink's fully erect penis nodded as well.

Oh Lordie, pudding and pie! It was huge, like an erect unicorn horn! *Fuck! He could joust with that shit!*

He grabbed a bottle of Nutego and unscrewed the lid *with a flick of his wrist.* The lid flew across the room like a Frisbee because it had been karate-chopped off by the back of his wrist. *Tae Kwon Brownie!*

"Let's break you in," he said as he pulled out yet another tub of Nutego. Because his dick is so huge it takes two full tubs to coat it with chocolaty goodness. "If I remember correctly, this wasn't one of your hard limits, and it certainly isn't one of mine."

"But what is it for?" I asked.

He unscrewed the lid and stuck his dick in it.

"Whoa!" I cried.

"Now, its time for you to lick it off," he said. The scent of milk chocolate with a hint of nuts filled my nostrils, and no, that smell wasn't just from the nuts that were all over his cock. I got on my knees.

"Mmmm…That's right Mistress Sterling. After tonight, Nutego is never gonna taste the same again."

I got on my knees and crawled towards him like an inch worm. I stuck out my tongue and clamped my eyes shut, not with eye clamps but with the force of my own will. *Ha! Girl Power is stronger than the metal bonds of genital and optic slavery!*

Mr. Pink chuckled.

I craned my neck out more, until the very tip of my tongue hit something…

Chocolaty!

I started to moan. Fuck! I loved chocolate! And it was hella close to my period too, which just made it taste even richer!

"Like that, do you?" I noticed his voice was a little strained.

Could I make it even strained-ier? I wiggled my tongue like the worm on the end of a fishing hook. *Time to catch me some chocolate covered cock!*

Chocolate smeared over my lips like edible lipstick. I nibbled, and then went back for more, diving into the chocolate sea of taste bud sensations. Chocolate flowed down my throat like a river, punctuated by whitecaps of frothy, salty, creamy seamen. I suckled his essential nectar as my blood sugar skyrocketed from too much high fructose corn syrup.

Oh God! The artificial natural flavors! The creamy sea of sugar and salt! *Well shit on a double crap stick!*

I put my mouth over the mushroom-headed hose poking out of his nut sack and began sucking and moving my head back and forth. It was kind of like a sea-saw, but I didn't actually leave the ground, and I did all the work. I couldn't get his pogo-stick into my mouth very far, because damn, it's hard to get something that big all the way in your mouth! So I just kind of played with the tip, but I didn't leave one, because it's awkward to tip you boyfriend for letting you suck his dick.

He fisted my hair. Tendrils fell around my face. It would have looked sweet if my mascara wasn't running into my eyes, making them red and black, and chocolate wasn't smeared all over my face as if I'd just been buried alive.

"Alright. That's enough, Mistress...fuck, what was your name again? Oh yes it was...fuck...uh...Sterling! Like silver. Mmmmm." He pulled my head off. "Now, it's time to rid yourself of that pesky hymen by plopping my anchor in your virginal canal."

"Don't plop it in so far that it will create waves!" I warned.

"Your cunt isn't as big as my ass. Not yet, anyway." Mr. Pink wiggled his eyebrows. "If you want, you can fist my ass tonight, after I fuck the shit out of you."

Oh golly gee. Goodness me. Maggie's first cherry popping. Should we put it on top of an ice cream Sunday?

"Carry me to the bed," I told him. I was ready to give it up for the cause—the cause being getting rid of my offensive virginity for reasons I didn't understand and didn't feel like asking about because it sounded like a long, traumatic story and I kind of wanted to keep things moving because *Antique Freak Show* reruns were on at 10.

He lay me down on the bed and I felt like it was a bed of roses the thing was so fucking romantic. Thornless roses of course! Because otherwise, ouchies! "I want to set free your Interior Goddess, Maggie."

"Interior Goddess? What the hell is that?"

He ran his fingers over my stomach. "I think you know."

"Well, I think she wants to be called something else."

"I'm sorry if those words upset you," he murmured.

"They don't upset me. They're just lame."

He grinned. "I only say them because you are my goddess. Because I want to worship you. Because I know you have a goddess inside you, and she has thoroughly captivated me. I want to draw her out." He moved down my leg, rubbing it, expertly. My muscles tightened and relaxed under his deft touch. "I want to touch her," he whispered reverently. "I want to kiss her feet." His mouth moved over my ankle, so hot on my cool skin. *I'm melting,* I thought. *I have to be. How could he feel so good otherwise?*

He moved up over me, his hands on my thighs, drawing up my skirt. Slowly, he spread my legs and his shoulders between them. "I want to hear her moan when I do this." He pressed his mouth over my silk panties.

I did moan. My legs reflexively tightened around his head. I felt his tongue, through the silk, dart out and touch my clit. It was wet. Hot. The fabric pushed against the folds of my skin.

"Do you think this devotion is lame, Maggie?"

I could answer. Even his words had a physicality that my body reacted to. His breath moved over my thighs, heating the areas where his lips once were, like a heat wave rolling across the great planes, killing all the air conditioners, and making them gasp out with dusty last gasps as they perish, forcing everyone to head out to the swimming hole because that was the only place left that was cool.

And his massive, hot cock was steering straight towards my swimming hole.

All hands on deck! It's gonna be a BIG ONE!

His lips were replaced by his dick.

SUDDENLY, A CAT JUMPS on Faythe's keyboard.

"Fuck! It was just about to get super hot!" Faythe cries, but before she can stop anything, the cat has already written Maggie's next line of dialogue:

zzzasasasasasasasasasasasasasasasasasasasasasasasasasasasn n n n n n n n n n n n n n n n n n n n n n n n n n n n n n n n n n n n n n n n n n n n n n n n n n n n n n n n n n n n n n n n n n n n n n n n n n n n n n n n n n n n n n n n n n n n n n n n n n

"Well, thanks for that, cat," Faythe says, then pushes Sir Fuzzybottom onto the floor and returns to her masterpiece.

THEN, MR. PINK TOOK me. He took me because that's all that he can do. Because that's all he knew how to do. Because he never

learned how to love, but just how to give and take, but not with love.

He was like that kid that makes his mother choose out his friend's birthday present before going to his party because he can't be bothered to think about what his friend might want. And his friend really likes it because his mother is a filthy rich slut, but the gift itself is meaningless because it came from the bowels of his hollow heart.

Bummer fuck!

His cock slipped into me, and my wetness slouched around us, like a sea of passion with no sand, because sand up your crotch itches like whoa!

Oh wait. Never mind. His cock slid into the saltwater bin right beside me. His hips thrusted up and down, and I could see dimples smiling at me in his ass as he humped the shit out of that water basin, causing so much water sprayed around us that I thought for sure he was gonna yell: *Cannon Ball!*

"I have to wash off all the remnants of Nutego before I take you, Mistress Sterling," Mr. Pink rasped. I guess that salt water was pretty freaking hot! And it was so hard for him to hump that hard that the vein in the middle of his forehead was humping too! "I don't want you to get a yeast infection," he explained.

Oh dearest me! He's so incredibly sensitive, thinking about my yeast infection before he fucks me! I smiled and playfully flicked some of the chocolaty salt water in his face.

Mr. Pink shoots back, bellowing: "Ahhh! AHHH!!! It's IN MY EYE!!! It BURNS!!!!"

"Oh! Double shit fest!"

He blinked a bit. Eyes red. Super red. *Fuck!*

"I just want to let you know before we start," he murmured, red eyes gleaming from salt water, voice low as a limbo bar, "I'm not into necrophilia."

"What?"

"I don't dig up corpses and fuck them," he told me.

"Huh?"

"I just want to let you know I'm clean," he said, planting his fists into the bed on either side of my hips as if he were planting trees. "I'm not gonna give you dick rot, or anything. So when I fuck you my dick isn't going to break off and burrow into your insides, muching on your organs as if they were beef jerky, and it won't turn you into a zombie, or impregnate you with pink hot dogs that will burst out of your stomach fully grown in six months and destroy the human race."

Judas kiss my ass! Someone pour some freaking holy water over these hot dogs! "I'm glad that's not gonna happen, but that description is oddly specific. Wait, do I still have chocolate on my face?"

"Oh yes, you do," Mr. Pink whimpered. "Mistress, do you want your little kitten to lick it off?"

Like hell I did! *Which actually means yes!*

He started licking my face. Then Mr. Pink flicked his wrists, and his dick started licking my cunt! Holy shit!

"I'm going to penetrate you with my penis now, and fuck away that repulsive virginity," he cooed.

"Yes." Why was my virginity so disgusting again? I glanced at the clock. Fuck! I couldn't think about something nasty like that at a time like this! *Antique Freak Show* was on in fifteen minutes! How long did it take to fuck? *Double fuck!*

Well, turns out it takes only ten minutes to fuck.

But holy fucking mother in Jesus *yes she's inside him now and her son is birthing her out and FUCK that is a freaking miracle!*

The entire earth shook. The bed was flying around the room like that children's movie that features a bed and also features broomsticks in some fashion I think. And he was twisting my nipples like the bedknobs that make the bed fly. *Holy fuck!* We heard crashes outside as half the city crumbled from the strength of our loin joining. *Super crap!* I whimpered against his chest, could feel his heart beating against my lips like the bass from music that is played way too loud *(but seriously, someone should tell those damn kids to shut the fuck up and get off my lawn! So it doesn't "belong" to me because it's a "park" and so it's "public property". You know what I say to that? FUCK! I have to look and listen to those little shits so get a fucking bulldozer and turn that park into a parking lot. See, you little shits? You ruin the fun for EVERYONE because you have to be so damn annoying! Now the value of my apartment just went down because it's located next to an industrial park instead of a woodland park!)*

His cock slid in and out of me, in and out, in and out. *Fuck!* It was going in so far and then it came all the way out. *Double fuck!* It went in further, until it was scrambling my ovaries, and then it came out, until it was tickling my pussy hairs. He grinned, calling them little pussy whiskers, and I was like, FUCK! Women who shave don't get to experience really touching moments like this!

His hips grinded my pelvis, like a meat grinder, and my pelvis was pink and raw. *Double Triple shit!* My virgin blood squirted out two minutes after we started, because my hymen was like a piece of rubber, and he had to pierce it with the retractable spike hidden in his dick to get it to pop. POP! It was so loud, like a balloon skewered by an evil clown at the birthday party of a little boy he didn't like because he told the clown his rainbow costume was shabby and the clown was like: *FUCK! I have to freaking wash this suit three times a day because little shit nosed fucks like you keep puking on it when I tell hilariously relevant political jokes!*

"That's it, Mistress. That's the sound of freedom! Now, ready yourself for some hard ass love!" Mr. Pink bellowed as the disco ball jiggly jangled above us.

God, that love was so hard on my ass, because I was on the bottom and my bottom was sore from the friction of the sheets on my sweaty ass. I don't think they were made of 100% cotton! My body shuddered around his pole of destruction as a wildfire spread through my veins. Then, the muscles deep inside my cunt, and deep inside other places, started to contract like a sea anemone that some nasty kid stuck their chubby finger into.

"That's your orgasm, Mistress Sterling! I'm gonna ride it!"

I started bucking against him like a fucking bucking bronco. In fact, we were bucking so fucking hard that the rainbow horsies on the ground started bucking too! My orgasm spilled out over all of us like nuclear fallout. I wiped my eyes with a glowing green hand that had just sprouted from my anal cavity.

"Fuck! Fuck!" The poet above me groaned.

"Rhyming fuck with fuck is just lazy, dude," I told him, because even though he was the poet, I thought he should be aware of such things.

"I'm ejaculating!" He cried, and hot cum shot out of his dick hole deep inside me, warming my insides like hot Nutego, and soothing the raging fires of the nuclear explosion. My green arm fell out of my anus and disintegrated, like so much dust because like whoa! There was a lot.

He collapsed on top of me, and my lungs collapsed. I started hitting his back and finally he rolled off of me, his dick rolling to the side of his leg like a limp tongue that had licked a banana slug and was now numb.

"I love you," I croaked, as the sweat cooled on my body, because really, what could you say after such an event?

"No. No, don't say that," he whispered, turning his face to the ceiling and scrunching it up in agony like a scrunchie a little girl throws away after her ex-best friend shows up to school the next day WEARING THE EXACT SAME ONE! *You're freaking lucky I forgave you for doing that to me, you nasty, backstabbing, cum depository Faythe!*

"Why not?" I asked, choking on how much emotion was bursting out of me. *Fuck!*

"You don't understand, Maggie. I'm incapable of love. I'm too dark, too mysterious, too tortured. There's no way a heart as pure and good as your own could heal my inner demons."

My eyes started to tear up. "But aren't you lonely?"

"Yes. But it is my lot to stand against fate with nothing but my own talents and determination." He nuzzled my shoulder. "Now, let's cuddle."

We settled down on his pink, heart-shaped bed, cuddling Pocahontas and Cinderella pillows. *Freaking yeah man!*

Mr. Pink flicked on the TV with a flick of his wrist. Then he flicked his wrist 500 more times to get to the *Antique Freak Show* channel, because he had like a million channels on that thing! I was like, hey, let's go get the remote control but Mr. Pink wanted to show off his super special skill. It was so hot the way his bones cracked as he flicked the shit out of that thing! Fuck!

Oh yeah, some lady had like a jar full of Abraham Lincoln's toenails that was worth freaking twenty thousand dollars! And some other person had a bundle of fart love letters that old freaking Irish dude who wrote *Ulysses* wrote to his wife or girlfriend or something that were worth like millions!

"Double crap," I whispered before falling asleep in my rugged, untouchable, lover's arms. Suddenly, those words had taken on an entirely new meaning.

14

T HE NEXT MORNING, I ROLLED onto the other side of the bed. Mr. Pink wasn't there, but there was a gigantic pink elephant lounging in the corner!

What the fuck! Is it safari time? Get my bazooka hard-hat, Billy, because the lions are circling!

Mr. Pink grinned at me. He was covered in a *pink*, mountainous, *pink*, amorphic, *pink*, gigantic cloth. *Well what's fit for the goose is fit for the gander! No giblets in the basket, please!*

Mr. Pink spread his legs wide. "Have you ever fucked a man in a snuggly, before?"

"Oh God. Nightmare fuel."

I could see his boner in the snuggly right between his legs. "I'm not wearing anything underneath this."

Sweet mother of Joseph! Can't. Un. See.

"That's right, you haven't fucked a man in a snuggly before." Mr. Pink chuckled. "This will be yet another first."

The snuggly was hot pink. Bibi doll pink. "I used to have a hot pink Bibi car this color," I said.

"Oh? Did you play with it often?"

I blushed. "Yes."

"Did it go fast?"

My blush deepened. "Yes."

"I bet you liked going fast," he whispered on my neck. "I bet you liked watching your hot pink Bibi doll catapult down the hill, her hair flowing behind her, wild and free."

"Yes." His hands were on my naked thighs, spreading them apart. I felt him, pressing up into my heat.

"Show me how fast you liked watching it go," he whispered at my neck, biting it softly. His snuggly-fied wrists wrapped around my back, fuzz sticking to the sweat on my naked body. "You don't have to hold back with me, little girl. Let loose!"

There was a little pink fuzz stuck to his cock.

I started to ride. He was right. As a little girl, I wanted to be like Bibi in her nice, new, shiny plastic car. I'd rolled her down the big hill next to my house, watching her yellow hair flow, watching Skippy, her little sister, bounce out of the back seat at the first turn and Tanya, her token African American friend, bounce out when she hit the pot hole. I wanted nothing more than to be like Bibi, flying so fast, so hard, so reckless and free…or I wanted to be like her until my dad ran over her car.

But I wouldn't think about now. I was on my own hot pink ride. Felt from the snuggly stuck to the base of his dick, catching on our juices.

"There's nothing as soft as a snuggly," he said. "It's gonna feel wonderful pressed up against your cunt."

And he was right. It did feel wonderful—*and* comforting, as if he'd dumped chicken soup in between us. It made me wanna fuck it so hard, so I did. And the soupy sex that pooled between us, lukewarm like it had been out on the counter for too long (but oh well, at least it wouldn't burn my tongue!), was just as comforting because it had been made with mama's love. I looked into his eyes and saw a possible mundane, bourgeois world that had nothing to do with the whips and chains of kinky sex, but rather the whips and chains of family—of boogers and dirty diapers, of stretch marks and baby fat that just seems to keep accumulating with each little brat you push into the world—*FUCK!* Nothing is hotter than thinking of pregnancy and giving birth while getting your brains fucked out!

Orgasm came after orgasm. It was getting a bit monotonous, these earth-shattering, mind-blowing, one-of-a-kind-but-not-really-because-I'd-already-had-ten-of-them orgasms! "Oh Gees!" I cried up to the heavens, as another ripped through me (Oops! That wasn't just an orgasm). He answered with a guttural "Ugghhhh!"

Anyways, my cunt, once again, sopped up his splooge like a sponge. *Where are the square pants, freaky yellow onion man?!?*

The snuggly was rumpled when I got off. My cunt was all fuzzy, and not just from my pussy whiskers. *Fuck! Like, double fisting fuck!* Why did something so bad have to feel so good? I mean, how could I continue to live in the mundane world after experiencing snuggly sex? It was so freaking snuggly!

Mr. Pink flashed a demonic grin.

A little thought drilled through my head like a bookworm, giving me a festering itch. "Wait a moment, why weren't you in bed this morning?"

"Oh, I was getting something for you." He nodded to the table in the center of the room, not to me. I glared at the table. What was so good about that fucking table? Especially since it wasn't table at all, but one of those fake oven kits that they have for little kids in daycare centers!

"The gift is on the table," he said.

Oh, so he was nodding for me to go to the table? Did that mean he wasn't overlooking me for the table? Or was that just what he wanted me to think? *Fuck! Triple fuck!* What should I do? There was a thingy on the table though. I decided to pick it up.

"Fuck!" I screamed.

Mr. Pink just grinned.

"I can't believe this? Is this what I think it is?"

"Yes," Mr. Pink purred. "Those are the actual letters James Joyce sent to Nora."

"No shit!" I cried out! "How did you know I totally wanted those?"

"I smelled your desire as we watched *Antique Freak Show* last night."

Well crap on a stick and call it a work of art! "Fuck! Are you like a weasel or some other animal that has a super sniffer?"

He looked down at his sweet ass smile. "I pulled off your panties this morning and pressed them to my nose. I took the scent of you in deep, until my lungs began to burn." He looked up at me, eyes dark with unbridled fire. *Oh my goodness!* "Your words might lie to me, Mistress Sterling. But your body can't lie. And the scent of you betrays your true longings."

Fuck! He could learn all that from my farts? But how could he afford what my farts resounded for? "Dude, this shit was expensive!"

"Money doesn't mean anything when you've got as much of it as I do."

Holy Cow! Score! Now I just had to think of more shit I wanted him to buy me! But before I could think of anything, my cell phone went crazy.

"What the fuck!" I screamed.

"Relax. Someone just called and left you a message."

I looked at my ringer. "No shit!" Then I looked at who had called. "Oh shit!" I said!

"What?"

Someone had called me from a payphone.

I only knew one person who still used payphones.

Triple Fuck!

I looked at Mr. Pink all bug-eyed and stuff. "We've got company."

15

MY DAD WANTED US TO VISIT. He wasn't really my dad, but just some bum that had lived on my mom's couch for ten years. You know what they say about feeding stray kittens? Well, the same goes for stray bums, although he came toilet trained so I guess we got a pretty good deal. My real dad isn't in the picture anymore. He's either a deadbeat, or dead, or is sailing around the world in an inner tube, or…who cares? He's not here, and he's not going to show up randomly or anything, so I don't need to think about his back story.

So anyways, my "dad" lived under the Suicide Bridge, which was handy, because it was on my route home from work so I got to see him every day.

My dad taught me everything he knew about cars, even though he'd never owned one. It is because of him that I became a mechanic. He also taught me how to drive, even though he doesn't have a driver's license, because *"I don't want to be registered with the man.*

That's how they catch you!"

Amen, Pops!

"How's mom?" I asked.

"Haven't talked to her in a while."

My dad doesn't have a phone so he and my mom communicate via his homing pigeon, JungleRat. JungleRat is missing an eye so my dad sewed a doily on it.

"Hey JungleRat!" I said and try to pet it.

JungleRat bit my hand.

"You know she's developed a taste for human flesh, dear," my dad reminded me. "Don't bother me, because my bloods' 200 proof whiskey."

I giggle, because I'm really fucking girlie and what he says is true. Someday JungleRat is going to start a zombie epidemic, and I'll be able to say: *I knew him when…*

"Damn, dad."

My dad nodded his head because he'd just taken a bite of something wrapped in wet tin foil, and he believes in chewing something at least twice before talking. "So Maggie, someone left half a burrito in the trashcan down the street. It's still warm. Do you want some?"

"Holy shit!" I yelled. "Score!"

My dad took out his handy, rusty Swiss Army Knife and tore apart that fucker.

I took a bite. Hot damn, there was nothing like lukewarm guacamole. I loved me some burrito. I never said no to a burrito. NEVER. Once, I saw a cockroach crawl inside my *Burrito Hell* burrito. Didn't even faze me. I picked up that fucker and took a god damn bite! Didn't even taste it!

"So, ready to go meet your man?"

I nodded. Ugh! My dad never approves of the guys I bring under the bridge. He's one tough cookie to please, that's for sure. Probably because he's such an old and stale cookie. He sends JungleRat after them if they aren't up to par.

Well, me and daddy-o were a-frolicking in the dumpsters when the limo pulled up and two meatballs (not meatheads this time, but delicious meatballs made with Italian sausage and eggs and parmesan cheese all balled up into hearty goodness) in suspicious suits popped out.

My dad dove across the bridge to a dumpster and hid himself. I kind of wondered why he didn't just duck into his own dumpster, but I guess the reason why is because my dad always insists on doing all his stunts and making sure the scenes in the movie detailing the story of his life are as dramatic as possible. It doesn't matter if no one will ever see this movie. It also doesn't matter that no one is filming this movie, or that there are no plans to ever film this movie, because all that matters is what's on your own heart. If the rest of the world doesn't want to watch or make your movie, just live the dream yourself! Fuck them!

"Dad!" I cried, picking up a fishing rod someone had left in the trash. I put a little bit of the burrito that had fallen from his hands on the hook and threw it in. Seconds later, I had a nibble and my dad had a new lip piercing.

"Maggie, my girl!" He sang. He loves his burritos too!

"Dad! Get down here!" I yelled. "I need to get that hook out of your mouth before my boyfriend gets here!"

"Maggie, shit!" He screamed. "I forgot! Those meatballs are here! The hot dogs are making their move!"

"What are you talking about, daddy?"

"Get away from them, Maggie!"

"No way! These are my boyfriend's best meatballs! They're really good at their job!"

My dad squinted. JungleRat began to circle overhead, looking for blood—looking for victims—looking for fresh meat.

I waved a broom at JungleRat. "Shoo!" I was the only one who got my boyfriend's fresh meat!

Oh wowie. I almost forgot! I'd just gotten FUCKED by the guy who was coming to meet my dad!

Awkward!

I glanced around all paranoid. Could I keep it together? Could I keep my cool? Or would I start to fall apart the moment I saw that tortured, deep soul who showered me with gifts and opened my cunt with lips that might have belonged to Adonis in another age, when people thought about that old man…whatever…*Götterdämmerung*! History was lame! Ugh, and that test was on Friday and…

I glanced over at the car. Then at my dad, stumbling out of the dumpster. *Triple fuck! Though not me getting triple fucked! Someone else is and I'm seriously freaking jealous, because I wish I was there instead of here with my old man and my new man about to clash like it's go time!*

Holy shit! I didn't remember much about the big bang from history class, but I was afraid that these two guys create another big bang! That couldn't be good! And holy Jesus mother fuck! Ever since I'd seen that documentary on String Theory like a year ago where they'd thought, for some inexplicable reason, that describing String Theory as someone playing a guitar was a good idea, I was seriously afraid the universe was gonna blow up every time I saw someone play the guitar!

Crazy purple shit! That you do not need! And if you keep it in your house, they're gonna call hoarders!

My dad started waltzing towards me like we were in a Jane Austen novel (even though her English peers probably weren't waltzing at that time, and no one waltzes in her novels). And something occurred to me. Something that bent the notions of time and space that I perceived at that moment.

How did I get here before Mr. Pink?

I mean, did the guy make me take the MAX line? The bus? Did he drop me off and circle around all creepy-like like JungleRat? What if he and JungleRat were part of some secret plot to completely destroy the world? What if they were going to make a gigantic universe-destroying guitar that the hot dogs were going to play?

My heart started to beat super fast because the thoughts in my head raced. The only thing that I could do to save our universe was to throw myself at Mr. Pink's feet, allow him to take me, body and soul, and hope that my bland, spineless, and feminine (because it was bland and spineless) love would change him!

But before I could begin to grovel, I saw my dad give Mr. Pink a slammin' high-five.

High what now?

"That's my boy!" My dad said, patting Mr. Pink on the back.

Shitsmacked! What in the *sacred name of Hog Dogs* did that have to do with anything? Did my dad know Mr. Pink? Oh my fucking god! Was Mr. Pink my dad's long lost son? Was Mr. Pink like my stepbrother or something?

All this time, had we been participating in the ultimate taboo?

The answer was, unfortunately, no. This book isn't that kinky.

"Wowie!" Said my dad, shaking Mr. Pink's hand. "I approve of this one, Maggie. He's a keeper."

I grinned, amazed at how fast Mr. Pink had won over my dad!

Mr. Pink leaned in close to sneak a kiss in front of my father. Full tongue. His hand on my tits, exploring them as if he were Christopher Columbus exploring the New World.

Oh my!

Wait! Daddy was still there! What was he gonna think?

And Mr. Pink's dick was totally busting out of his pants! *Crapola!* But god damn, it was so fucking hard and huge, and I wanted to ride it!

"It's alright," he whispered against my neck. "I brought him Tequila."

My eyes began to water. Something caught in my throat. *God damn fleas that sprinkle off JungleRat like dandruff every time he flaps his wings!* I gagged and coughed out a few more fleas on Mr. Pink's shirt. Luckily Mr. Pink was too caught up in this romantic moment to notice that, or the flies circling the trash heaps, or kids yelling out of their car windows as the cars zoomed past on the bridge, or my dad pissing on a chalk drawing kid had made in the middle of the street.

"God damn, you're so sweet," I whispered. *So sweet I want to grab that left over burrito, shove it up your ass and fuck you with it!* He knew just what my dad had wanted! My dad always said his best friend was booze! What a thoughtful gift!

"Let's blow this popsicle stand," he said.

Right. It was sex time. "Bye dad!" I yelled

My dad didn't notice. He was too busy arguing with his other best friend, the stop sign. I giggled. Silly daddy!

Mr. Pink pulled me back into his world of darkness and leather— i.e. the back of his leather upholstered limo. "It's time you fulfill your destiny, Mistress," he whispered.

A chill shot through my skin, and as the doors to the limo were shut by one of his well-seasoned meatballs, I realized that something about my body was changing yet again.

16

"OH NO!" I CRIED. Once we got into Mr. Pink's dungeon, my cheeks were as pink as...as pink as...I looked down. Oh Lordy me! Could I really say it? They were as pink as something down there...

I clenched my eyes shut and my hands shut. "I'm on the rag!"

Mr. Pink frowned. "So?"

"So I'm all bloody! I can't get freaky now!"

Mr. Pink lifted one of his brows. "Well, that all depends on how freaky you want to get."

"Wha??"

He glanced down at the red strawberry pooling in my previously white panties. "I fucked you till you bled last night. And even after you bled, I still fucked you."

Wowza! His words ran through my body like daggers of feral pleasure. My cunt growled!

Mr. Pink frowned. "Did you say something, Mistress?"

Yowza! What should I do? I could feel my cunt gearing up for more! All that talk of getting fucked had really got the blood running, almost as if my cunt were a great mountain and he'd caused an avalanche by yelling up into its cavity: "Tally-Ho!"

He stepped forward. Ripped off my shirt.

"Hey!" I slapped his hand. "That was from the $5 bin!"

"I'll buy you another $5 shirt. Hell, for you I'd buy the entire bin!"

I was about to slap him again, but them I remembered those letters. *Yes, the letters!* I fluctuated to the memory. Fuck! This guy could buy me like a million $5 bins! "Oh, Mr. Pink!"

"Now where were we? Oh yes, there's nothing more erotic than a girl on her period," he murmurs, kissing my shoulders, working his way up to my neck. "The scent of the artificial, 'floral' chemicals in your shampoo mixed with your body's iron."

"Well, when you put it that way…"

"It's like your cunt is crying blood for me, as if it knows my pain."

My heart had a seizure. "Awwww!!!!!!!"

"It's true," he said. "When a woman's pussy bleeds, it makes me want to worship it, because I know that it is crying the bloody tears I've kept up inside ever since I was a little boy."

Fuck! That was so deep! And he was so freaking tortured! Still, I didn't want to ask him any questions, because I didn't really want to watch him crap blood out of his eyes. *Tear duct constipation, man!*

"You're not gonna need to be lubed up, because you're already ready." He unzipped his pants with a flick of his wrist. *God, okay, I kind of feel weird bringing this up, but like the first time he did that trick it was kinda cool, but now it's just weird. I mean, it sounds like his bones are breaking and it's right before he fucks me. I can see this getting old REAL fast.*

He slipped the head of his dick inside me.

Whoa! Me forgetty clicky-clicky!

His cock glided right in. I squished my cunt around him. "Holy hot dogs!" I moaned.

"That's right, Mistress Sterling. Are you ready to process my meat?"

"Fuck yeah! My cunt is a little meat grinder!"

"Mmmmm," he murmured. "You're like a defrosted cabbage, all slimy and moist. But you're hotter. No ice has crystallized in even the furthest, unexplored corners of the cave betwixt your quiet cove. I've already scalded them into plumes of steam with my rock-iron love."

Fuck! Steam was rising out of my cunt, and it moaned like a freaking tea kettle about to blow! *Well fuck me in the ear!* Blood dripped down my thighs as his cock pushed in, further. Each stroke sent ripples of blood out of my sweet bud of awakened desire. *It's red tide! And Jesus Christ! It smells like all the fish just died down there!*

"That's right, Mistress. Command my body with your desire! Mount my cock!"

I pushed him onto the floor and started to bob up and down on his dick, as the crimson evidence of my lust spread between us like contaminated chicken noodle soup. *Double botchulism crap!*

My claws dug into his arms as I pinned them above his head. I waved my head around, foaming at the mouth.

"That's right, Mistress. Let out your Interior Goddess! Let her howl at the moon!"

My orgasm was mounting inside me. It always mounted before it exploded. And fuck, my cunt was like a swollen blister. *Someone get a needle and sterilize it with a lighter because I don't think I can hold on much longer!*

I threw back my hair, wet with my sweat. It stuck to my neck. I felt him caress my face with his fingertips as I opened my mouth in a silent scream.

"Dominate me. Take me back into your womb. Make me a part of you, Mistress. As you shed your life's blood upon me, let me give you my life."

"FUUUUUUUUUUUUUUUUCK!" I screamed. "I MEAN HOLY FREAKING FUCK!!!!!!!!"

Blood bubbles burst in the space where our skin fat slapped together. His wet balls jiggled near my ass crack. And I came, right then and there. I came as if my body had been designed for sex, just as it had been designed for eating and sleeping and breeding and eventually dying. I came and surrendered myself to the darkness that spread over us. He was mine. My beautiful, dangerous, dark lover. And I was his as well. For we had both given ourselves to the other, and now there were no secrets between us, and the rest of the world did not exist.

Well toot on my horn! There's nothing like a good nihilistic orgasm to start the day!

"Fuck. I think we need to take a shower," Mr. Pink said, looking down.

Holy hot dogs in hell! Our bodies were pink! Well, mostly rusty and dark red but...let's just call it pink.

I blushed. "Some got on your snuggly."

"That's alright," Mr. Pink whispered. "When you're out during the day, I'll snuggle up in it and look down at it and touch it, and be reminded of one of the most beautiful moments of my life."

"Awww!" I said. It was one of the cutest things I'd ever heard. Also, one of the most disgusting. "Let's get in that shower, bro!"

WE GOT OUT OF THE SHOWER and lay down on the bed. "So what is that?" I asked, pointing to his unicorn keychain.

"That's the most important thing in the world to me," he said.

"Huh?"

"Seriously. Without this, I am nothing."

"What do you mean?"

"Remember the first time we met?"

"Huh…" I thought back real hard. No, I couldn't remember, but shit! This had to be real! Right? I mean, we had to have met at some point because we were here together and…Triple fuck!

"I told you my business secret," Mr. Pink explained.

"Oh yeah," I said, even though I had no idea what was going on. No seriously, what is going on?

"I told you that in the middle of my business deals, I slap my junk down on the table and give everyone such a fucking manly stare they can do naught but bend to my will."

Oh yeah…Shit! Mr. Pink was such hot shit! *Hot pink shit!*

"Well, before I do, I reach inside my pocket and touch my unicorn. In a reassuring way, not a pervy way."

"Thanks for clarifying. That really puts me at ease," I said. Fuck, did that make me sound like an easy girl? Was I an easy girl? Like over easy eggs?

That last thought reminded me of just earlier before, when he'd scrambled my ovaries with his penis spatula. God damn! I touched my tummy. The pan was still hot! I looked to Mr. Pink. I was going to need more olive oil or else my eggs might stick to my pan!

I leaned over Mr. Pink. "You know," I whispered, running my hands along his tanned, muscular (but not too muscular) shoulder. Yes, both of those hands were running over his fucking incredibly sexy shoulder. I wished I could freaking knead his dough-ball muscles into little balls and then let them rise a little bit. Hmmm, I'd put them into the oven and bake them at 350 degrees for an hour and a half! Then, I'd take them out of the oven—wearing my muffin mitts, of course, with little happy bears having a sparkling birthday party!— let them cool for fifteen minutes, then take out the butter and butter them up so I can eat them!

Oops! But then where would Mr. Pink's muscles be? In my tummy! *Double whammy fuck face! FUCK SHIT!* Then…that would make me a….*cannibal!*!!!!!!

17

Interior Goddess...ready to ramble again...ugh...

MY FACES RISES ABOVE the white-capped ocean like a moon. My heart washes ashore with broken seashells. It longs. It bleeds. It beats. But before my final exhale, it shall stop.

In the past, whenever I have tried to overcome the struggles in my life, I tell myself to take a deep breath and wait a moment before acting. If it's a difficult task, I focus on taking just one more step, and then one more, until I finish. If it's some sorrow I must bear, I focus on taking just one breath, and then just one breath more, until the tumultuous pain that sears my soul settles like mist over the sea. And sometimes, at night, I lay awake and listen to my heartbeat to remind myself that I'm alive.

But these simple things I take comfort in—one more step, one more breath, one more day—are lies.

One day you will take your last step. It won't matter how close you are to your goal, you won't be able to make it. Your body will collapse even if it is just one more step away.

One day your heart with beat its last beat. And as you listen in silence, like you've done so many times before, you'll realize that this is it. The muscle has worn out. It can't even pump one more time. One last time. It won't matter how hard you will it to keep going, even if it is just for one second more, because it will stop

One day, you will draw your last breath. You won't be able to take another, even though the act is so simple, and you've done it your entire life until that point. You'll open your mouth and try to suck in air, but your lungs won't inflate. And slowly you will suffocate, as your mind vainly chants: One *more breath! Just one more! It's nothing! I've done it so many times before…*

This is my sorrow: That my human body has a limit, and no matter how much you dream, or beg, or will, you will not overcome it.

There are things that are too beautiful for this world—things that cause our bodies to burn up, like a moth devoured by a flame, when we get too close. For it doesn't matter if that beauty is just one step, one heartbeat, one breath away. It is unattainable. Out of reach.

Failure is our destiny.

18

ID I WANT TO EAT that sexy man's brains? *His brains would be pink.* FUCK! Was it a sign that I was destined to eat them? *But everyone's brains are pink.*

Well, golly gee, that complicated things! *But hey!* Everyone in the world had pink brains. And Mr. Pink's name was pink. Did that mean that Mr. Pink secretly wanted to eat everyone's brains? Had I unwittingly stumbled across his master plot to suck the brains out of everyone's heads with a silly straw?

Fuck! I loved silly straws! How could he *taint* them with his nasty pink man-eating crap?

Wait. Wait. Hold on cowboy! *Freaking yank that horse to shit!*

Mr. Pink liked horses. I mean, let me put this another way. Considering his Unicorn Secretary and this my little horsie collection, I think that what he felt for horses went a little beyond just 'like.'

And wait. There was something else. Think! Think! Put your thinking noggin on!

Alright. Horses were animals

Birds were also animals.

Fuck! Fuck! That's two fucks, or a 'double fuck'!

Animals. Birds. The day I'd met Mr. Pink, birds had flown by his window. Biblical birds.

Triple fuck!

I knew a bird. JungleRat! JungleRat was the opposite of a biblical bird. He was a freaking street pigeon with a missing eye! He'd soiled some grandmother's doily that took her like freaking three months to make (because holy shit it's hard to make those freaking doilies!) and stuck it in his bloody eye cavity! Top Conspiracy Theorists universally believed JungleRat would be the cause of the zombie apocalypse.

Quadruple fuck!

Zombies. Eat. People. Zombies are cannibals with seriously fucked up skin. Mr. Pink had perfect skin. Almost too perfect. ZombieRat had the worst skin I'd ever seen on a bird. I mean, FUCK! I could see it! My skin was also nice. *No! Stop thinking about skin! You were seriously just on to something there.*

Right. RIGHT! *Oh my god.* I'd figured it out.

Mr. Pink was a zombie.

Five-sync-septal-tubble-pebble fuck!

The My Lil Horsies. No! My Little Zombies! Bronies! Brozies! *Fuck brains!*

Oh God! The room was Pink!

That could only mean one thing.

I was inside a zombie brain.

Oh shit! Mr. Pink's name was pink. When I first got that agreement I had to sign in his office, the writing had been pink but the rose had been black. Why wasn't it pink? *Fuck, no! I got it!* When I addressed the envelope I'd sent the nondisclosure agreement in, I'd used *pink* ink to write his name but...*black* ink to write mine! *Oh shit!* Black was darker than pink! Black marker ink could go over pink marker ink, but pink marker ink couldn't go over black marker ink.

Sixth-times-a-charm-bracelet-not-a-charm-that-would-be-nice FUCK!

But wait. My name was Sterling, not Black. But wait! I didn't know who my father was! What if his last name was Black? What if, for my entire life, everyone had been hiding my secret identity from me? What if they'd named me after silver because they wanted me to feud with gold, but in truth, gold hadn't been my opponent all alone! I was the color who could swallow up both those colors and turn them into me! I was...*black.*

Head just exploded fuck!

I was the black rose. He was the pink, brain-eating psycho. It was my destiny in life to assassinate him. If I didn't, the planet and all life on earth would die!

Oh! It would have all been so easy! Why did I have to fall in love with the man I must destroy!

But wait! Wait! Maybe there was hope. Mr. Pink loved horses. *Especially unicorns!* Maybe he really wanted to be innocent again! Maybe there was a way we could turn back the clock! Maybe our hearts didn't have to beat so fucking loud! Maybe everyone misunderstood! Maybe the hot dogs only wanted to make everyone cannibals because it was more disgusting to think about what was going into a zombie's mouth than what was inside your hot dog!

They just want to be eaten! *Oh, hot dogs! You don't have to make everyone in the world zombies just so we will be willing to eat you again!*

Mr. Cannibal Zombie Masochistic Psycho took out his unicorn keychain and dangled it before my eyes.

No! Must not give into the sparkly! Don't hypnotize me! *God DeMint! Why did it take all the way until now to remember the evil, master plan of the hot dogs!*

19

The Interior Goddess Speaks!

N O. NO! DON'T DO THIS to me! Seriously don't! I mean, this story almost had a plot. It almost had a plot, people! You can't dangle that funky carrot in front of me and then yank it away!

That's it! I've had enough!

God! I hate this story! I DON'T WANT TO BE HERE ANYMORE!!!!

Yeah, reader. You think that you are suffering right now because you have to read this? Do you really think your pain can compare to mine? You do? Well, you know what? You're *wrong*!

Because *I am stuck in this story.*

Because *I don't have an existence outside of this story.*

Oh God! It's so awful! Because *no matter what I do, I can't leave!* I can't even kill myself because I don't have a will outside of the author's, and for some reason that fucking sadistic bitch has decided to keep me in here!

No! No! Don't turn the page! Please! Help me! HELP ME! Get me out of here! Don't leave me here alone! You don't understand! No! NO! Please!!!! Please!!!! I'm in such pain! Please! Don't walk away! DON'T WALK AWAY!!!!!!!

I just want out.

Please!

PLEASE!!!!!

Please........

Faythe America:

SO, YOU FLIPPED THE PAGE. You left her there, crying out in agony. You decided to read this book, even though each time someone reads one of the Interior Goddess' passages, they conjure her soul. When they remember her character, they rip her from the blissful darkness of unconsciousness. Each time you do this she awakens and must, again, relive the horror of being in *Fifty Shades of Pink.*

She wants it to stop.

More than anything, she wants to escape this reality.

But she can't.

To do so, she would have to have stopped this book from being written—from being read—from being remembered. Or, she'd have to destroy every person who has ever read the book, and erase its existence.

She can't do that, though, for an ebook is not a physical object.

Once something has filtered its way into the bowels of the Internet, it is there forever, rippling through electro-waves of cute kitty pictures and porn through our eternal, free, unrestrained consciousness. Even if it were pulled from retailers it would still exist —in someone's email, on a torrent site, or in that small section of your brain filled with things you wish to God you could forget but never will.

Her true goal is to destroy civilization and mankind so she can, once and for all, destroy herself and *rest in peace.*

But she is a phantom of the text, so she'll never be able to achieve her goal.

Cackles as lightening flashes!

That's right! Read her section again! And again! And again! Drink in her pain! That heady mixture of blood and tears and helplessness that makes you feel powerful! *That makes you feel alive!* Revel in it, and partake in the gluttonous, apathetic, majestic ennui of the gods! For only when things suffer *hopelessly* and *beautifully* do desensitized and alienated beings such as us find meaning in life.

You think you're different? Do you really think you can put this book down now, after discovering what it is really about?

I don't think you can, because you're pretty fucking evil.

Just like me.

20

I GIGGLED AND GRABBED Mr. Pink's wrist. "Oh fuck! Your unicorn was dancing!" Mr. Pink looked down on me with affection. "There's my Mistress with glittering teeth!"

"Fuck?" I screamed at him like a hissing snake that can also scream. "My teeth are glittery?"

Mr. Pink nodded. "You're shits are probably gonna be glittery tonight, too, because I just sprinkled a shit load of glitter into your mouth just now!"

"What? You did?" So *that* was why it felt like a swarm of bees had just erupted in my lungs. "Why did you do that?"

"You were having bad memories."

"Oh!" I said. "Well, thank you, then."

He looked at me a long moment. There seemed to be little else to do in long moments. "Look," he boomed, kicking that long moment to shit, "even if I have to kill you, I'll dig up your corpse, and I promise to never fuck or sleep next to another woman again."

"WHAT?"

"Never mind," he said. Then his pants started gyrating to an awesome techno beat. "One moment. I have to take that call."

Crapers! Craper-Daper! Did he have to take his pants off to talk to people on his cell…?—oh wait, no, it had just been on vibrate and had been located in his pants.

"Yellow," he said.

Holy fuck! He was so damn cool. I wish I'd thought to greet people by saying colors over the phone. Red fuck! No, blue fuck! Pink fuck? No, I could only use that greeting when I talked to Mr. Pink. Then I could say: Pink! Hi Mr. Pink! Whenever he called. Fuck! Awesome idea! Totally gonna do it if I remember! Maybe I should write it down or something…

Mr. Pink slam dunked his cell phone. Oh wait, billionaires probably don't use flip phones. I mean, he touched the screen on his phone and it went to a screensaver of floppy eared bunnies riding around on top of horses with little birthday, sparkle hats on! "I've been called away on urgent business. I must leave the premises. Wait here for me, Mistress. You can punish me for leaving in the middle of our…interesting afternoon…when I return."

"Fuck, does that mean I just get to stay here?"

"Yes. You may." He rasped. I don't know why he was rasping at this moment, but at least he wasn't rapping! "I want you to start to consider this home. In fact, you can even use my comb. Or write a poem."

"Poem isn't a full rhyme with comb and home. It's like, an eighth rhyme or a sixteenth rhyme."

His eyes blazed with untamed passion. "Fuck, you're incredible. God. I just want you to take me now. Tell me all the things I've done wrong. Fuck. I want to stay here for you to make me your bitch."

That sounded pretty cool, but seriously, I was like getting tired and stuff. I just wanted to curl up under the battle-scarred snuggly and read James Joyce's ass poems. Mr. Pink could wake me up when he came back, and both of us could fall into the thrall by the scent of raw, fresh passion.

Hell yeah! Then it's gettin down time!

My eyes blazed. *I think we need a freaking fire extinguisher in this room!* "I'll wait for you, dude. Go slam your dick on that document. Seriously, I want you to throw it down so hard that it breaks the table in two!"

Mr. Pink nodded. "I'll do my best for you, Mistress. If I don't manage to break it in two, I'll stick needles through my dick."

I frowned. Fuck shit! That was a little harsh. "That's ok. I'll just, like, horse whip you, or something."

He neighed.

Fuck! I mean, okay, I like horses too, but just HOW into horses was this guy?

"Ta-ta, Mr. Pink."

He stumbled. Bit his lip. Fuck, now I could see why it was sexy! When you bit through your lip, blood leaked down your chin making you look like a vampire. Vampires were totally in, right? Oh yeah! Mr. Pink was such a fucking rock star fashion stud! Then again, with a name like pink, he gotta be!

I started gnawing on my lips super hard. If Mr. Pink was going to tease me so rigorously, I needed to step up my game. *I'm gonna blow a bubble with my puss, dude!*

Mr. Pink gagged. "If you keep doing that, there's no way I'm gonna be able to leave, my little wood-polisher."

Oh! God! *Just wait till he meets my beaver!*

"Hurry back!" I said. *Heel—no, I mean HELL yeah! Look at the size of that bubble!*

He saluted me and my nipples perked up like good little soldiers.

I squished my arms together to rub my tits against each other in hopes that would swallow the swelling need that was gathering in my breasts like mother's milk, but FUCK! It did little to dampen my need, probably because my need was already so fucking damp.

But other than that, I simply watched him step away.

I watched and did nothing.

I could not help him, where he was about to go. Into that cold, ruthless world of insider trading and backroom deals. I did not know what Mr. Pink had to do in the world to stay on top. To have the money he needed in order to have a secret lair and millions of horsies and everything else he possessed. He said he could buy the whole world if he wanted.

But was that really what he wanted?

Was Mr. Pink the sweet, innocent unicorn, frolicking in the valleys of vast, green forests and sparkly shit? Or was he the dark, tortured man, who would spend his life grasping for phantoms in his doomed search for happiness, as he decimates everything around him that he might have loved, had he not been so blind to his single-minded, self-destructive ambition?

And God! More importantly, which one did I want him to be? The sweet-natured, happy, content, loving hippie, or a sociopath who could buy me everything I wanted?

Double sparkly sociopathic fuck!

Oh well. Didn't have to answer that now. Fucking Bubble Boy was on!

Fifteen minutes into the show, I realized something. Something that might hurt Mr. Pink's chances of karate chopping that desk apart with his dick.

He'd forgotten his unicorn key chain!

21

M R. PINK HAD ALREADY taken the Pinkmobile. *Well fuck some crap!* Okay, I guess since it was his car, that wasn't too surprising that he took it. But that meant the only other car I could take that freaking Volva I'd tried to build myself like building a car was some arts-and-craft project you'd do at girlie scouts.

Well, excuse me! I deserve three buttons, because building a motherfucking car is a lot harder than planting a fucking tree (but still not as hard as starting a fire with twigs)!

I jumped in front of my car. Maybe, if I scared it a little, it would be-*thefucking*-have. And that totally didn't look like 'behave' even though that was what I was going for, but rather 'be' and 'have', which are often the first words that you learn how to conjugate when you learn a foreign language.

Fuck! Was the car trying to speak to me? What language did it speak? Wait, the key wasn't in the ignition! It couldn't speak! Was it trying to sign language at me? Fuck, it couldn't even move without the key plugged in!

Well I decided to put an end to its silence by *getting the fuck in* that car. I popped off the door.

No, that wasn't a typo. I didn't pop the door, I popped it right the fuck off! God damn, was this thing street legal? Wait! Since when did I care about what the street thought of me? It was made of fucking pavement! Not flesh and blood! Fuck!

"You can't fool me, crazy street! Taste my burnt leather! I mean, my burnt rubber!" Fuck, I needed to get leather wheels so I could whip mouthy sidewalks when I drove up on them! *Teach you to talk back to Mistress Sterling, bitch!*

Well, fortunately I was on my way, but unfortunately, I'd forgotten to do the most important thing! (Which was listening to what my car had to tell me.) What she was about to tell me was that she was about to break, but unfortunately I didn't get it until she'd already fallen apart.

I jumped out on top of her carcass and started beating my chest. "Why!" I screamed up at the sky. "Fuck, now you're gonna rain, too? Why don't you just—"

"Stomp on my dick!" A voice next to me yelled.

I looked over. Damn, that guy was smokin hot! Walking around with his shirt off! In nothing but his boxers! His caramel skin had caramel dripped all over it! *Sticky fun yum!* And his eyes…fuck! Just the way he looked at me, I could tell he was a real man.

"Get over here!" He said, marking an ex over his bare chest. "This baby's so hard the rain evaporates when it comes within six feet of it."

Fuck! So damn hot! My life with him would be perfect. But wait, who was he again? And why did he look so familiar? "Hey, who are you?" I asked.

"What? You gotta be kiddin me, Maggie babe! It's me, Jonas!"

I stopped dead in my tracks.

Jonas.

I tapped my thinking pointer finger to my thinking bubble, careful not to tap too heard so it wouldn't pop. *Jonas, Jonas...*I thought and thought as my head started to pound from being prodded so much by my insistent finger.

Oh, right. Jonas. My best friend. The guy I always told all of my troubles too. Who, after listening patiently for hours, and letting me use his favorite shirt to clean my two snot-holes from crying so hard and long, always bought me ice cream, or new shoes, or tickets to the opera. Fuck! Jonas! Who was always telling me I deserved better than assholes who treated me like shit! OH YEAH! Jonas!

Suddenly............

.......suddenly, suddenly.............

...........................*suddenly*.....................................

....

....

....

....

.........all those sexy thoughts about him, and me, and forever, all disappeared, because that guy was, like, embedded in the 'friend zone.'

"Hey!" I yelled. "Dude, you came at just the right time. I have to get to Mr. Pink ASAP!"

"Why do you need to go to Mr. Pink?" He asked. "Why is it always Mr. Pink instead of me?"

"I don't know!" I yelled back. "I mean, fuck. Why did my car have to break down in the middle of the street? Why is everyone honking their horns at me? Why is a fucking grocery bag flailing in its death throes in the wind the most beautiful thing anyone has ever seen? Why? WHY? Fucking hot dogs!" I yelled, my voice blaring over the horns.

"Hot dogs?" Jonas asked.

"Look, it doesn't matter. I need to get to Mr. Pink. *Shit* is about to go *down*, and he needs me. So take me there now!"

Jonas put his hand on my arm to stop me. I guess he could have also done that to give me a message, or to push me, or to smear something sticky on me and then run away giggling because he was a practical prankster, but he decided to stop me with it. "I wish you would run to me the same way you are running to him. I wish you would…feel certain things for me."

"What things?" I asked. *Fuck!* How long was he gonna hog the spotlight? The relationship between me and Jonas was all about me and my feelings. Me and my wants. Me and my neurosis. Why was he trying to get me to listen to him? Just because he was my best friend and everything? Fuck that shit!

Wait! Maybe he was just worried that I was going to like try to jump his bones and make a freaking xylophone with them. *Bedroom black metal! Fuck, who borrowed my cowbell? I'm looking at you, rotting Christ!* "Dude, it's okay!" I grinned. "I just don't really see you in a sexual way, you know? You're my friend."

"Fuck!" He yelled.

"My bentest—I mean, bestest—friend in the hole world!"

"That doesn't mean we can't be together! I mean, we can still be best friends!"

I shook my head.

"Oh God!" he cried. "After all these years of following you around...I mean, I turned down a full ride to Harvard so I could follow you to Community College! I spent a year getting stoned off my ass in Amsterdam! I learned four different languages while we were there, so you could talk to the locals and make friends! I translated conversations for you that went on for hours and consisted entirely of:

Oh my God, he didn't!

Oh yes he did!

No way!

Yes way!

Shit!

Fuck, I know.

But seriously, oh my God, he didn't!

I LOVED you!"

I looked at him. "What?"

"I said, I love you," he declared, taking my hands. "And I want to spend the rest of my life making you happy. I want to dedicate my life to your happiness. I want to make love to you, Maggie."

My heart melted. No, wait, he'd just gotten some of his caramel on my chest. *Need a napkin, dude!* Wait, no, he was saying something important! Something really special. I was feeling something. But was it love, or acid reflux?

Here was a guy who wanted to make love to me! Who loved me!

But...but...there was also Mr. Pink. A man who was incapable of love. A man who was bat-shit instead of kind. A man who'd once said: *I don't make love. I hump. Hard.*

And shit, no one could make you happier, or hump you harder, than a man incapable of love.

I thought back over what Jonas had said. Wait, something there doesn't make sense. *Something was a little creepy.*

I gave him my best accusatory glare. "Wait Jonas. Did you say you *followed* me to Community College? I thought you turned down that Harvard scholarship because you *really* wanted to do pottery with me."

"Come on, Maggie! Obviously I followed you there! They *have* pottery at Harvard!"

Well crap on a potter's wheel and watch it spin around! No, wait, both of us took that class. Double crap!

"I don't know why you think 'following' me is okay, alright? That's fucking creepy stalker behavior! I mean, sure, Mr. Pink stands in front of his computer monitor and watches me sleep every night via the hidden camera he tacked above my bed, and he stuck a tracer chip in my skull so if I ever tried to leave him he would find me. And yeah, sure, that chip is wedged into the area of my brain that controls my motor skills, so if I ever tried to remove it I'd end up paralyzed, and then I'd never, never, *ever* be able to leave him."

Jonas' face was no longer red. It was white. "Oh my God, he did that? Maggie, listen to me, that is seriously fucked up. You can't see that guy anymore! I mean, fuck! I think we need to call the cops!"

I balled my hands into fists! How dare he talk poorly of Mr. Pink? He was just jealous, because he wasn't as sexy or successful! "No, Jonas. Mr. Pink is just worried about my safety, okay? Do you know what's fucked up? Giving up your dreams just for a chance with a girl, you creepy psycho!" I swallowed. "Besides, we can't date. If I did, and we broke up, who would comfort me?" I explained to him when he frowned. "Now, BFFM, that's Best-Friend-Forever-Man, alright? The traffic is jammed all the way across the bridge because of me.

How will I ever make it to him now?"

Jonas started to weep very manly, restrained tears. Or maybe he was just holding one in a big one.

That's just another reason why I love Mr. Pink, I realized. *We don't hold anything back from each other. If we want to express our feelings through our 'other mouth,' we do, and partake in that language only those desensitized connoisseurs can savor.*

"Do you really love him?" Jonas asked.

"Yes," I said. I mean, we'd fucked like three times already, and once on my period. If that wasn't love, I didn't want to know what was.

Jonas sighed. "Alright. I'll be here for you now, and forever, but when you and Mr. Pink break up, I think I deserve a pity fuck."

Pity fuck? Well, isn't he cheeky! *Mmmm…Wonder what he wants me to do to his ass cheeks. Maybe his real name is maroon. Or black and blue. Oh wait man! Golden grape fuck! He's 'friend' material, NOT 'boyfriend' material!* "I'll consider it," I mused.

His eyes lit up. "Really?"

"Yes. I will really consider it."

"Wow. I never thought I'd hear those words from your mouth!"

I pressed my hand over his mouth as he started to lean in for a quickie. *Gotta be slicker than that, slick!* "I said maybe. In the future. I will consider. Now, how are we gonna get me out of here?"

Techno music blasted from the speakers of one of the nearby, angry cars. Jonas flexed his pecks to the beat. "Tell me why I should help you if sex isn't a guarantee."

"Because you're my bestest best friend after Faythe—!"

"No. A real reason. That weird ass guy has moved your heart." He grabbed my hand and stuck it over his chest. "Now you have to move mine."

I bit my lip. *Double dummy!* I mean, the reason why might embarrass Mr. Pink if it ever came to light. What if Jonas let it out that Mr. Pink was only such a fucking stud because of a unicorn toy?

But if he doesn't have that toy, today, at the meeting, he might be....*impotent!*

"Look," I said, pulling out the key chain. "I have to give this to Mr. Pink."

Jonas raised his brows. "Uh, that's it? That fucking girl's toy?"

"You don't understand! This isn't just a toy to him! Unicorns are to Mr. Pink what spinach is to Popeye!" God! Why wouldn't the world understand! Why did I keep using words to describe things? Ugh! I hate words! It takes so much time to say shit! Time that could be spent doing things, like falling on my face!

Oh my dearest me! That reminded me of Mr. Pink, and how I totally fell in front of him. That busted lip was the beginning of our tender love.

"Please, help me Jonas! You're my only hope!"

Jonas rolled his eyes and his hands in his mouth and let out an umpire whistle. Oh wait, umpires already have, like, whistling tools that are called whistles. Well, like how an umpire might whistle if he lost his whistle, unless, of course, umpires have lost the knowledge of their ancient art form of whistling. *Damn, regular whistle tools! We were losing our ability to whistle on our own with you around!*

Anyways, Jonas totally still possessed this ability.

Just then, a white horse flew over the bridge. *Whoa! Double crap! Hope it's not horse crap, though!* It stopped once it reached Jonas, and put its white, beautiful nose against Jonas' totally fab abs.

"Your ride awaits, my lady," Jonas said.

The horse took one look at me and shook hits head, hiding its nose in Jonas' armpit.

"Come on, Jelly Button! You have to let her ride you."

The horse shook itself.

"No, she's a very special girl! You have to treat her nicely!"

The horse gave me a weird look again.

"Dude, I don't think your horse likes me. And why the fuck do you have a horse?"

"This was my great grandfather's horse. And my great-great grandfather's horse. She's been in the family for generations. Hell, she practically raised me. She's the closest thing to a mother I've ever known."

"Fuck. I didn't know that."

"Yeah, well, not everyone thinks that horses are fit to raise children," he said.

I squinted. "Fuck that's deep."

"It's real shit, man."

"I know."

"No, by your foot," he amended.

"Oh crap!" I jumped away.

"I think she likes you," Jonas said, grinning.

Really? She'd just tried to take a dump on my foot! "I think that actually means she doesn't like me."

"Oh, come now." He petted the horse's nose. "Now, you treat her well, you hear? If everything goes well, she might give me a pity fuck." He turned his attention back to me. "Alright Maggie. Time to hop on."

"Uh, am I supposed to ride this thing alone?"

"Yes," Jonas said.

"But I've never ridden a horse before."

"It's really easy," he said. "Just scratch her left ear when you want to turn left, and her right ear when you want to turn right. When you want to stop, say, 'don't go eaten all my jellies, yo!' and she will stop." He licked his finger and held it up to the sky. "Fuck. If you don't leave now, the meeting's gonna be over!"

"Shit!" I screeched. Guess I had no choice but to *ride the pony*!

22

S O I WAS TOTALLY RIGHT and Jonas was totally wrong. The horse hated my guts. Guys are often like that, you know? I mean, sometimes they are right, but sometimes they are wrong too. But still, I think this is an important issue to bring up. However, the philosophical quandary that question posed was certainly less pressing than the teensy, weensy problem I faced at that moment: How the FUCK to get off a *crazy ass insane* horse!

I mean, alright. Last night, I had said that I bucked like a bronco. But there was no comparison! This thing bucked like a nest of angry wasps that were really freaking angry! Like each one of those angry wasps was bucking! Like you were a little wasp flea on one of their backs and had to hold onto them while they went berserk, trying to kill everything around you! It was climbing on cars like it was in a music video!

Ding-dong!

Every time I scratched its right ear it went left. Every time I scratched its left ear it body-slammed (or is it torso slammed? horsy slammed?) me into a Merabies. Fuck! I hated those damn luxury cars! Like freaking luxury crackers! Only taste good when you put them with fancy ass cheese! On their own they taste like wet noodle cardboard!

And then it saw some kid eat ice cream.

Oh man hole fuck!

Its nostrils flared. It bared its teeth. It blew air through its lips, and while that may sound pretty innocent to you, trust me it isn't! There's nothing freakier than watching stale, horse-breath air blow through a horse's thin lips! It's like watching a sheet dry on a laundry line on a windy day! Only it's a horse! Fuck! And while you may not think that's too freaky, that kid totally agreed with me.

The little shit screamed, her pigtails flying up towards the sky as if they, too, were praying to God to help her. But *He* didn't listen. No one did, as the horse charged forward, beady, demonic eyes locked on that ice cream.

The kid seemed to notice the horse's single one-on-one obsession with her freaky sugary cone and threw it up into the air. The horse leaped up to get it, clearing her. The ice cream fell on its head.

Shit! Now what?

The horse freaked. It wanted that ice cream more than anything else. It wanted that ice cream so bad that it went crazy. And this was a problem because that ice cream was so damn close, but yet so far away! I mean, I could have reached up and given it to the horse, but I was too scared because an essential part of my character was being too scared to do anything when it was convenient for the plot!

Anyways, eventually we somehow reached the pink tower. Probably because the pink tower was pink, and white horses freaking love that color. Also, towers. Saving damsels in distress is ingrained into their blood. They had to do it so much in the Victorian's romantic reimagining of the Middle Ages that they fucking charge towards pink towers every time they see one at this point, similar to how baby birds know how to peck out of their eggs, or recently hatched sea turtles know to haul ass towards that ocean.

But God damn! Enough about sea turtles! I wasn't a freaking crustacean! *Fuck! Triple crap fuck! Cut myself on an oyster shell!* How was I going to get inside?

Only one way! I leaned forward and used my thinking brain super hard.

Okay. When I scratched its right ear, it went left. When I scratched its left ear, it tried to fucking kill me. The tower was on my right. *Fuck!* How could I do this?

Wait, maybe if I scratched its right ear twice, it would go left, because two lefts make a right!

Hell yeah! That's just fucking science! Or math! Or something!

Feeling like hot shit, I scratched that right fucker.

Only I'd just realized I'd forgotten my lefts and rights.

Triple shit!

The horse cackled. *Fuck! I didn't know it could do that!* And raced towards the window of the tower.

FUUUUUCK!!!!!!!!!

The horse jumped up on top of a love bug and leaped over the newsstand, the hot dog stand, and the little old woman who was standing with her walker, through the window.

Her pink hooves kicked down that window.

Glass flew everywhere! Kind of like glitter, but this was glitter that could make you fucking bleed. Glitter that could fucking kill you. *Hardcore sparkles, man! Someone sacrifice a pineapple! Fuck! We put pineapples and hot dogs on pizza now! Hawaiian doggie style with extra cheese, XL, be there in forty-five!*

The horse landed on the table. Right on top of Mr. Pink's special legal documents.

Mr. Pink looked up. "Unicorn," he whispered.

Um, what?

Wait! *Holy shit!* When the horse had mowed through that kid eating ice cream, the cone had gotten stuck to its forehead. It looked like a unicorn! Alright, so its horn wasn't solid gold, but it was solid waffle cone! And do you know what? After everything that had happened, it seemed a little magical.

Double heartwarming crap!

I glanced at Mr. Pink again. He looked…sad….*but he freaking loves unicorns! And horses! What the Hell?*

"Oh Maggie," he whimpered. "Oh, glorious waffle-cone unicorn. Never in my life did I think I'd see such beauty. Why did you have to come to me now, in my darkest, most humiliating hour? I am not worthy!"

Huh?

That was when I saw the man next to Mr. Pink.

He had his dick out, on the table. Fuck! It was huge! I mean, no where near as huge as Mr. Pink's, but he had the goods to back up that smug look on his face. Fuck face! What was wrong with Mr. Pink? His junk was so much junkier! Why didn't he flap that shit out?

Oh yeah, unicorn key chain! He needed his sparkly spinach! But… what kind of compost would come out if the unicorn ate it instead? Well, since it had a waffle horn, probably waffle flowers! *Fuck, I want some now!*

The other man was looking over at Mr. Pink. "It looks like today is the day the great Mr. Pink finally falls! Hahahahaha," he cackled softly, rubbing his hands. "All great men must step down some day, Mr. Pink. You burned too brightly, too fast. You're all burned out! The company is mine!"

Holy crap! Shit was going down!

The entire company? Oh no! If Mr. Pink didn't slap his dick down...

"Now, will someone please get this fucking horse out of here?" The man with his dick out yelled. "This is an important business meeting. I don't believe we should let the plebes in!"

Plebes? No! I was Mr. Pink's important special somebody! Mr. Pink should totally tell that asshole off!

I looked at Mr. Pink. He had his head in his hands.

Fuck! Sparkly spinach! That's why I rode the fucking horse here. "Mr. Pink!" I shouted as men started to surround the waffle-unicorn. I grabbed the unicorn key chain from my pocket and threw it to him.

His eyes perked up. He stood, closing his fist around the unicorn. Then he put it in his pocket. "This meeting isn't over yet."

All the men who had been circling me stopped. The man with his dick out started to shiver, and his dick shrank a bit, no longer engorged from the knowledge that it was sure in its victory. "What do you mean? You didn't whip it out! You didn't— "

He unzipped his pants and slammed his cock onto the pile of legal documents. "That girl, over there, is my bitch. You got a problem with that?"

Mr. Pink picked up his dick again and slammed the fuck out of that table. *Fuck! His dick was like a freaking HUGE meat cleaver!* It broke the table in two. It shred the legal documents. They spun around him like confetti, and the glass all around the room reflected his dick.

The other man cried out, his dick retreating into his pants. "Please forgive me, sir! I did not know! I did not understand!"

Mr. Pink smirked as he looked at me. "I trust the table is broken to your satisfaction, Mistress."

"Fuck yeah! I'm freaking stopping at the grocery store to get more Nutego!"

Mr. Pink glanced over at the man he'd just epically pwned. "Remember this the next time you meet me one-on-one for a business transaction. And remember this: My dick gets bigger with every victory, and I've never lost."

Fuck! How the hell was I going to be able to take it in my cunt if it kept getting bigger?

"Now, Miss Sterling. My attendants shall escort your magnificent steed and your magnificent self to my private quarters. I'll send someone out for Nutego and, when we meet again soon, don't go easy on me, or my ass."

23

I LEFT MR. PINK'S PRIVATE quarters. I couldn't stay there. Not any longer. I went outside instead, to the streets, to the people, to the plebes. I let Jelly Button ride off into the sunset alone, or rather, she just took off when we got outside. Oh well. Jonas would find her. Probably.

Goodbye, Jelly-welly! You hated me, but you saved my most beloved person! How will I ever thank you? How about I don't, because you really freak me out.

I sat down on the sidewalk and waited and waited until freaking finally "Mr. Important" decided to show his face.

He crouched beside me, his shadow eclipsing mine. "Maggie," he whispered, taking my hands. "You came, riding in on a white unicorn, my goddess of strength and beauty, my savior."

"Uh, yeah. That's me." *Triple fuck!* It wasn't me! I wasn't a goddess! *Downgrade down to double fuck!* How could I say what I needed to say next? *Ugh!* There was no good way to do this! I cleared all the phlegm out of my throat the words I'd been holding back erupted from my mouth: "I can't do this anymore."

His bottom lip wiggled. "What?"

"I just can't."

"You can't what? Find the Nutego?" His eyes began to water. "I said I'd send someone out to get it for us—"

"No, that isn't it!" I interrupted, my voice to sharp, my cheeks hot, my throat closing as if some invisible first were wrapped around it. "You know what I mean. I can't *do this*. *With you.* Not anymore."

"But why? Maggie, I…."

"Stop. Just stop. It doesn't matter what you say. I don't want to hear it."

"Why not?"

"Just because! I mean, holy hot dogs, do I need a reason? I'm poorly written! The plot demands it!"

He stared at me, unshed tears twinkling along his bushy eyelashes.

"Fuck, do I really need to explain this? There needs to be a cliffhanger to set-up book 2, and if there isn't enough demand for a book 2, then there still needs to be a cliffhanger so that the author can share her pain from not making enough money!"

I stood. He stood up after me, grabbing my sleeve. "But I thought this book didn't have a plot!" He bellowed. "I thought this was written so average women could live out their fantasy of being swept off their feet by a billionaire vicariously through you! It's my job to shower you with gifts! To give you hot, incredible, unforgettable sex! To reveal my deepest, darkest secrets that I've never told anyone before, because despite my steely exterior, inside, I'm a pure, pink puffball!"

I looked away.

"Come on, Maggie. Wasn't the sex incredible? Let's go fuck. Let me love away your worries…"

"I know the sex is incredible! God, it's fucking amazing!" I spun around, hair whipping across my face. "And you're amazing too, but it's just not that simple! You and I can't just be together because we love each other and have hot, incredible, unforgettable sex!"

"Why not? Hearing you say that makes no sense!"

He reached out to me. I slapped him away. "I already told you! It doesn't matter how we feel! The plot demands it!"

"But…why? Why? Maggie, please tell me!"

I turned away, unable to look at him any more. "Sequel bait."

The admission left a bitter taste in my mouth. My stomach recoiled. My head pounded.

He stepped back. "No," he whispered. "No. I won't believe it."

"It's true," I croaked. My eyes burned from unshed tears. "We have to stretch out the story as long as possible so we can make more money!"

"But readers hate cliffhangers! Why make people wait months and months for the ending?"

I slapped away his hands. "Do you think I don't know that? Do you really think I don't understand what you're saying? I know cliffhangers are awful. You hate them. Readers loathe them! Especially when the author holds back answers just for the sake of getting them to buy the next installment, like what the fuck was going on with those hot dogs, whether or not you're really a zombie master or just fucking insane, and why the Interior Goddess is even part of this story!

"I know cliffhangers are awful! I know this, in the cavity in my skull that should house a brain, but in reality just contains clichéd reactions to clichéd scenarios. Even though readers hate them, and know the author is just fucking with them, they can't help but give in, *because they're invested in the story!*"

"No!" Mr. Pink cried. "People won't fall for such a cheap emotional trick!"

"Oh, they'll rage, but they'll buy the next one, even if we price it at...*$12.99!*"

"No, don't say it! Don't abandon your values! Think of your fans!"

"I know!" I cried, falling to my knees. I tore out my hair and raised my fists to the sky. "An ebook should never cost that much...*BUT THEY DO!!!*"

Mr. Pink collapsed beside me, holding me in his arms, and our hearts beat as one, furiously, staggeringly, painfully, trying to stand against our fate.

"Don't do it," he whispered, lips caressing my hairline. "I love you!"

"I can't help it!" I wailed. "I'm just so...*poorly written!*"

"No. You can't let the author do this to us! You must fight against it. Force her to acknowledge your feelings!"

"She doesn't care about my feelings!" I slurred. "Because she's a *fucking sadist* and so are the people who consume mass media! No one wants to read a story about two people who just have a good time because happiness is boring! *They only read to watch us suffer!*"

"Why? Why are they so mean?" He whimpered. "I just want happiness with you! A boring, uneventful, happy life! That's all I want! That's all I've ever wanted!"

"It can never be," I whispered. "I mean, shit, look at how she's treated us already! All you want to do is cuddle in your snuggly and play with unicorn dolls, *but she made you a fucking corporate takeover artist*! She made me a car mechanic, *but I don't know anything about cars*!"

He leaned back. "No."

I rolled over, crying. "It's true. My love of cars defines me, especially since the fact I love them proves I'm not just some simpering girlie girl but an independent, thoughtful, unique woman. But do you know what? *She didn't even research anything about being a car mechanic before she wrote me!* So I look like a *fucking idiot* because *the car I built broke down and I couldn't fix it* even though *it was my pride and joy*. I mean, fuck! MY LIFE'S WORK BROKE DOWN AFTER FIFTEEN MINUTES!"

Mr. Pink waved his hands in the air even though he totally cared. "Oh, say it ain't so!"

"It is so! And you know it because...*she wrote you that way too!*"

"No. I won't believe it. You're not just a Mary Sue who works as a car mechanic to show that she's different even though she has absolutely no knowledge about cars! Show the author that you're more!"

I take a step forward, and fall on my face.

"No, not that way! Show her you're a flawed, interesting, perceptive being, not just a loveable klutz!"

"But I can't! My clumsiness is my only flaw! If it wasn't for that I'd be completely...*BLAND!*"

"No. You're more than that. I know you're more. Your interior goddess..."

"Is just some crazy crap the author cooked up? Do you even know what that means?"

He swallowed.

"See!" I yelled. "We say things and even we don't know why we're saying them, or what they mean! And even though we know we're being a ridiculous caricature, we can't stop! *Oh God, I'm trapped in this nightmare and there's no way out!*"

"Fight against it! Hold me, baby. Together, we can do anything! Take comfort in our love, the only thing that's real in this world!"

I held him, but I found no comfort in his arms. "Oh God! Is this love between us just a lie?" I wailed.

"I can't believe it. I feel for you so much. Just put your hand down my pants and feel how much I feel for you!"

"That doesn't mean you really love me! You don't know me! Do either of us really know each other at all? We don't even know ourselves! We don't even have character!"

Mr. Pink fell over onto the sidewalk. "Oh God! Get me out of here! Wake me up from this nightmare!" He reached out to me, his hand opening and closing in a futile fist again and again. Or maybe he just wanted to twist my titties so that we could make the bed spin around again.

But there was no bed! *Double hot pink shit!* There was nothing but this emptiness! Unable to take any more, I ran away. And he just watched me run, screaming "NO!", even though he was totally a faster runner than I was, and could have caught up with me.

And, perhaps, the greatest tragedy was that he couldn't even force himself to get up and grab hold of the thing that he loved most in this world, because the plot had already determined it would be best for me to look away and, even though my heart was breaking…

…*to never look back.*

EPILOGUE

FAYTHE SET DOWN her pen. *Damn*, she was good. Who wouldn't want to dominate a CEO in the fastest growing corporation in the world while he wore a snuggly? Snuggly sex was fucking hot. *And fucking genius*, she congratulated herself.

But what was up with all that weird stuff at the end? Why did her character say she was 'poorly written'? Faythe had bled and sweat and cried for these characters! She loved Maggie as if Maggie were her real best friend! What had they meant when they'd said they had no true motivations…?

You know what? Fuck it! Fuck motivations! *You do what I say, bitch!* Faythe thought. Besides, characters in fiction didn't really have a real life, right? I mean, it wasn't like they were self aware.

But still, they had some good suggestions. Had to give them props for wanting to end on a cliffhanger. Also, $12 ebooks? Faythe cackled with delight!

Just then, Maggie burst through the door.

"Dude," Faythe said, swiveling in her chair. "You will not believe how much work I just got done. It has the most incredible ending I've ever made, if I do say so myself. You see, the main character—"

"We broke up," Maggie whispered.

Faythe spun around. "What?"

"Mr. Pink and I. We broke up."

"What? Why?"

"I don't know. Oh God, Faythe, why does it hurt so much? What am I gonna do?"

"Oh sweetie…"

"I just…" she threw herself into her pillows. "I just want to die!"

"Then why did you break up with him?"

She shook her head, and then stuffed it back into a pillow. "I can't talk about it! It's too horrible to even talk about!"

"That makes no sense."

"I know! Nothing makes sense anymore! *I* don't make sense! Why do I have to exist? Why was I even created? WHY???"

"Oh sweetie." Faythe moved over and rubbed Maggie's shoulder. And as she did, she wondered why Maggie's tears sounded like an endless stream of golden coins clinking into her pockets…

THE END

ABOUT FAYTHE

Faythe America is the author of the inimitable parody *Fifty Shades of Pink*. Her favorite food is apple pie, her favorite drink is generic, cheap beer, and she sleeps under an American flag quilt her grandmother Eberhard sewed for her while recovering from rabies. As a result, Faythe is terrified of small, wild animals, and especially squirrels. She has taken it upon herself to police their population by digging up their nuts and burring them in other places. And that's probably more than you ever wanted to know about Faythe America, but in case it isn't, you can find out even more about her at http://faytheamerica.com.

Printed in Great Britain
by Amazon.co.uk, Ltd.,
Marston Gate.